Word Learning
Word Making
Word Sorting
50 Lessons for Success

**Ready-To-Go Lessons
That Help K–2 Readers and Writers
Learn Key Strategies**

By Judy Lynch

SCHOLASTIC
PROFESSIONAL BOOKS

New York • Toronto • London • Auckland • Sydney
Mexico City • New Delhi • Hong Kong • Buenos Aires

Dedication

To my brother, Larry Ingram. As a pilot, he doesn't know anything about teaching reading, but he knows everything about loving his little sister!

Acknowledgments

To Dr. Judith Neal, California State University, Fresno. Her continuum for teaching visual-word analysis is the framework for this book. Her clarity about literacy learning is appreciated by all of us lucky enough to learn from her.

To Bev Ruby, my Reading Recovery teacher leader and dearest friend. You are always there to "think aloud" with me about literacy and life.

To Carolsue Acres and Julie Bills, long-time teaching friends, who gave me important feedback in the early stages of this book.

To my editors at Scholastic Inc., Wendy Murray and Joanna Davis-Swing, who patiently waited for this book while life (football games, graduations, and the time I needed to let my soul catch up) was happening to me.

To those teachers I have been privileged to teach with in the Rio Linda Union School District and especially my "family" at Madison School. We work in a culture where ongoing teacher education is valued and expected. I am honored to be learning with you.

And especially to my dear family: Mike, Michael, Shannon, and Kevin. Writing takes time, which is a precious commodity for this full-time teacher. You understood when I disappeared into the office upstairs and you (usually) ate take-out dinners with enthusiasm. You know I love and adore you all!

Cover design by Emily Waters

Interior design by Sydney Wright

Illustrations on page 53 and 99 by Yvette Banek; other interior illustrations by Amanda Haley

Cover photo and photos on page 6, 11, 26, 40, 47, 116, by 121 by Doug Niva

ISBN: 0-439-20578-6

Copyright © 2002 by Judy Lynch

1 2 3 4 5 6 7 8 9 10   40   08 07 06 05 04 03 02

Contents

Introduction

As a full-time teacher, I've found it useful to take current research on how children learn words and look for practical applications. There are many methods of primary-level instruction, besides worksheets and skill and drill, that can promote the acquisition of the graphophonic knowledge and decoding procedures beginners must acquire to become competent readers (Ehri, 1998). The lessons in this book will focus on word learning while reading because "reader's eyes come to favor words as the units that are most easily processed" (Rayner and Pollatsek, 1989). These word lessons are meant to support the guided reading and shared writing lessons a teacher is already doing.

Working with very young readers, we have all seen children who can read only whole words like their name or the logo of their favorite hamburger franchise. How do we move them from this stage to eventually looking at the details of print in multi-syllabic words while reading increasingly more difficult stories? The process of word learning happens in broad phases (Ehri, 1991; Neal, 1999). Generally knowing at what level my students function helps me to plan lessons appropriate to the needs of a class, small groups, and individuals. I designed this book to complement your literacy lessons and to focus your instruction based on broad word-learning stages. My hope is that the lessons you choose here will help you zero in on what your students need to know.

Stages of Word Learning

This book is designed so that classroom and support teachers can choose word-learning lessons arranged from easiest to most complex. A variety of researchers have labeled this "word-learning development." Prominent currently are Ehri's (1991) phases: pre-alphabetic, partial alphabetic, full alphabetic, consolidated alphabetic, and automatic alphabetic. In simpler terms, I like the broad continuum of teaching for visual-word analysis described by Dr. Judith Neal (1999):

Use of whole-word units
Beginning use of sub-word parts
Use of embedded letters and letter clusters

Whole-Word Units

Early on, students recognize whole-word units like their name and a few high-frequency words, such as *the*, *I*, and *mom*. For the classroom teacher, this is an ideal time to teach one-to-one correspondence as students match their pointing finger with gross units of print. We want students to read and write the words they know in a variety of contexts. If they know the common word *the*, we want to make sure they can read it in different books and in different fonts, and write it with ease. A core of well-known, high-frequency words allows for more fluent reading and serves as a basis for learning how words work.

Sub-Word Parts

From the very start, children can use their developing knowledge of letters and sounds to read words in simple patterned stories with clear illustrations. Students initially use picture clues to decode the new word in the pattern. Gradually, they grasp the details of new words, noticing sub-word parts: initial and final consonants; suffixes like *-ing*, *-er*, and *-ed*; and, finally, common word patterns that they can learn to "chunk."

Embedded Letters and Letter Clusters

To become efficient readers, students need to recognize and use embedded letters and letter clusters in words. To do this, they must focus their attention on the inner letters. More complex consonant patterns, such as *scr*, and vowel patterns (long vowels and diphthongs) challenge new readers. Using analogy (taking something the child knows to help her figure out something new) to decode words containing these features is more demanding because "it is harder for the child to work with consonants and rimes when more letters are involved, and also when the spelling pattern does not have a direct letter-sound correspondence" (Clay, 1993).

How to Use This Book

After a short chapter that contains mini-lessons and activities for teaching the concept of "word," subsequent chapters follow the broad continuum suggested by Dr. Judith Neal, moving from whole-word units to sub-word parts to embedded letters and letter clusters. Do not feel as if you must march through these lessons in order. Instead, select the ones your students need, as determined by your observations of their reading and writing. The lessons will supplement the instruction already going on in your classroom. Often they will provide a 10 to 15 minute focus on word learning that you can use in conjunction with a shared reading, guided reading, or interactive writing lesson. You can use the lessons in the morning with the whole group or throughout the day with small groups that need more focus. I have scripted most of the lessons so that you have a model to help you get the flow and

hear some of the precise language I've found helpful to use with my beginning readers. Please read through the sequence but make the wording your own, adding your own style and personalizing the lessons for your students. Above all, remember to make clear to your students what they are learning and why. We don't want confused students like the first grader who confided to a classmate: "My teacher always tells me to sound it out, but I don't know what that means. I just move my finger and my lips, 'cuz she does. Please don't tell her. I should have learned that in kindergarten." I have built into the lessons the opportunity to teach, model, and then practice each skill so that you can monitor students' understanding of their word learning.

Lesson Format

Each lesson has the same format. The top left corner indicates the chapter the lesson is in. Under the title of the lesson, you will find the grade levels it is most commonly used with and the approximate time it takes to complete. You can quickly read the purpose of the lesson under Focus and see which materials to gather. The sequence of each lesson is:

Teach: You model the basic skill or strategy, thinking out loud as you go.

Practice: Students practice the new word-learning strategy as a group.

Follow Up: Students apply what they have learned and perhaps extend it to other contexts, with the careful coaching of the teacher.

Using What You Know: This section links the lesson focus to the regular reading and writing that is going on in the classroom.

Chapter 1

What Is a Word?

Experienced readers know what a word is. But for kindergartners, those whose first language isn't English, and many beginning first graders, the concept of a word may still be a mystery. Although they have heard spoken words since birth, they hear them simply as a stream of sounds. As a teacher of beginning students, I have to be aware that some children may not realize the sounds they hear can be broken down into smaller units, such as words, syllables, and phonemes. When I show them print in a Big Book, in a poem in the pocket chart, or while writing a morning message on chart paper, I point out where each new word starts and discuss why we have spaces between letters. This practice helps students to realize that the stream of sounds they hear in speech is actually made up of distinct units—words.

The lessons in this section help to foster students' awareness of words as separate units of sound. They can be used with a large group or small groups, depending on students' needs. I generally present them to the whole class first and then give extra help to those who need it in small groups of two to six students. Use only enough lessons as needed, then move on.

Quick Assessment

You can use a modification of Marie Clay's *Concepts About Print* test to see if students can distinguish the difference between words and letters. I do this quick check after a few weeks of group work, during which most students grasp the concept of what makes a word. This assessment identifies students who need extra help in small groups.

✓ Materials

1. Simple book with a single line of large print and good spacing between words.
2. Two three-by-five-inch cards for each child. Show students how to hold one in each hand and open and close their fingers over the line of print. (I tell my students that it is like the automatic doors that open at the grocery store.)

Directions

✓ *Close your cards.*
Now show me just one word.
Close your cards. Now show me two words.
Close your cards. Show me just one letter.
Close your cards. Show me two letters.

I like dogs.

like

like dogs.

k

do

✓ Evaluation

It is important to ask about both words and letters because young students often confuse the two or call them by the same name. Any child who can't identify all four items in the assessment will be pulled into a small, temporary group for further instruction.

Bean Bag Toss

GRADE: K–1	TIME: 5–10 minutes

FOCUS: To teach one-to-one matching between spoken words and a concrete object (the bean bag)

Materials

✳ A bean bag or small stuffed animal

Sequence

Teach

I like to do this as part of the morning routine on the rug:

> *When we talk to each other, we speak with words. Sometimes we talk so fast that it is hard to tell. Today I am going to talk very slowly so you can repeat what I say. To help, I will use my bean bag, tossing it one time for each word I say. Let's try it with Sarah. Come up here, Sarah.*

I take turns using students; they love to have the class repeat a sentence about them.

> *Hmmm, let's see what she is wearing today. Okay, now listen carefully to what I say about Sarah so you can repeat it. <u>Sarah has a pink sweater.</u> Now let's say the sentence together, and for each word we'll gently toss our bean bag to another person. Watch out—it might be coming to you!!*

Model gently tossing the bean bag to students and saying one word for each toss. Then have the group join in.

▷ **Tip:** If students are confused by multi-syllable words like *sweater*, explain that some words have more parts when we say them (*sweat/er*), but they are still one word, one thing, for example, *Sarah's sweater*.

Practice

Repeat with other sentences about other students, being sure to include their names.

Follow Up

On chart paper, write a sentence or two that you used for the bean bag toss. Stress to the group that between each word you are putting a two-finger space (hold two fingers up to the spaces between the words) to separate the words we say. Reread the sentences together with different students coming up to use the teacher's pointer to touch under each word.

Using What You Know

Read a familiar Big Book or poem line by line to the group. After each line, have the group repeat the line as you toss the bean bag for each word.

Word Hop

> **GRADE:** K–1　　**TIME:** 5–10 minutes
>
> **FOCUS:** To teach that each word we say has a match to a word in print

Materials

* "Humpty Dumpty" page 12 (first line of the nursery rhyme); enlarge one set of cards to use as a model and make copies of page 12 for each student

* "Mary Had a Little Lamb," pages 150–151 (for extended practice on two lines); enlarge one set of cards to use as a model and make copies for each student

* Any familiar nursery rhymes: Put the words of the first line or two on five-by-eight-inch index cards to make more practice sets (one word per card)

Sequence

Teach

Begin the lesson like this:

> When I read, I read one word at a time. To help practice that today, we are going to use the first line of "Humpty Dumpty." Remember <u>Humpty Dumpty sat on a wall</u>? Let's all say that together—<u>Humpty Dumpty sat on the wall</u>.
>
> Let me show you the words that go with it.

Show the enlarged word cards to your group, reading each one aloud before you place it on the floor.

> Watch me. As I say each word, I will step on it and hop over the spaces. The spaces on the floor between the words are like spaces in a book; they separate the words to make it easy for us to read each one.

Model the process; then have a student or two copy you as everyone says the line.

After the demonstration, send students off to work individually:

Now you are ready to do your own. Remember, there is a space between each word card.

Practice

Pass out individual sheets of "Humpty Dumpty" to each student. Then have students follow these steps:

* Cut out the words.

* Lay out the word cards on the floor in the proper sequence with large spaces between the words (use teacher's sample as a model).

* Step on one word at a time, saying the word (slowly at first, then a little faster as students hop on the word cards using alternate feet for each word).

* Push the words a little closer together and repeat. Discuss how the space shows that a new word is next.

Follow Up

Use "Mary Had a Little Lamb" (see pages 150–151) to repeat the process, but now include two lines of the nursery rhyme. This is good to do a day or two later or with a small group that needs further guided practice.

Using What You Know

Use poetry you already have in your pocket chart to "stomp for each word." I invite my students to sit on the floor with their knees bent and feet flat on the floor in front of them. Together, we say a familiar line of a poem we are looking at in the pocket chart and stomp alternate feet, one for each word we say. This is the next level of difficulty after hopping on the actual word card, and it further reinforces the one-to-one match of what they see and what they say.

Humpty	Dumpty
sat	on
a	wall.

Word Learning Word Making Word Sorting: 50 Lessons for Success *Scholastic Professional Books*

Counting, Reading, and Writing

GRADE: K–1 **TIME:** 5–10 minutes

FOCUS: To teach the match between the words we say, the words we write, and the words we read

Materials

* Sentence strip
* Pen and scissors
* Pocket chart (optional)

Sequence

Teach

Begin the lesson like this:

> *When I want to write a sentence, it sometimes helps me to count the number of words that I will write. For example, today I want to write The fireman came to visit. Let's all close our hands and count the words on our fingers. Say it with me slowly: The fireman came to visit. How many words is that? Let's check our fingers.*

Help where needed to explain that *fireman* is only one word.

> *That's right, now I know that I have five words to write. I'm going to write my five words on a sentence strip. What's the first word?*

Model writing each word and then going back to reread what has been written to generate the next word. I also point out the two-finger space I use to separate the words to make them easier to read.

Practice

Begin the guided practice like this:

Let's all read my sentence to see if I wrote five words.

Check for the match to the words you and the class had put on your fingers and written.

Now watch me as I cut the words apart. Say the sentence with me as I cut the words.

The whole group repeats the sentence as you cut out the words, starting at the beginning of the sentence. Put each word in the pocket chart (or chalk tray) after you have cut the whole sentence apart. To begin with, spread the words apart to emphasize spaces. Each time you reread the sentence, move the words closer together and talk about the fact that each space separates one word from the next—just like in a book!

Follow Up

After guided reading with a small group, it's useful to write about the story you have just read. With emergent readers, you can do this by writing a sentence containing the pattern of the story (for example: *I like to eat___, I can_____*). As students write their own sentence in simple journals, put their words on a small sentence strip (a regular sentence strip cut into quarters) and mix it for them to rebuild. They can take this mixed-up sentence home in a small envelope and rebuild it again for homework.

Using What You Know

In journal writing or writer's workshop, I ask emergent writers to say their sentence slowly and count the words they will write on their fingers. I show them the spaces between their fingers and remind them to put spaces between the words as they write.

Word Boxes

> **GRADE:** K–1   **TIME:** 5–10 minutes
>
> **FOCUS:** To teach the concept of a word in writing and spelling, using a one-to-one match with markers and a box for each word

Materials

* Word-box boards, one per student and one for the teacher; use the template on page 16
* Markers (beans, pennies, or any other small manipulatives), six per student
* Overhead projector or chart paper and pen (optional)
* Overhead transparency of word-box board if using an overhead projector (optional)

Sequence

Teach

I usually do this lesson with a small group because of the manipulatives, but you can do it with the whole class. Begin the lesson like this:

> When we are writing, sometimes it is hard to tell how many words we are going to write and where to put the spaces between words. One way to solve this problem is to say the sentence we want to write very slowly, word by word. To help us learn how to do this, we use word boxes to show us how many words are in our sentence. Let me show you my word boxes.

Your word boxes can be on an overhead transparency, drawn quickly on chart paper, or put on the word-box board the students will use. Continue.

> We have been studying George Washington this month (or any current topic of study), so let's see how many words I say about him. <u>George Washington was our first president</u>. Watch me as I move a marker into a box for each word I have just said.

Say the sentence again and move a marker into a box for each word.

How many markers did I use? Six? Let's count them and see. Good, that means I have six words to write and I have to remember to put a space between each word. Now let's have you try it!

Practice

Pass out a word-box board and six markers to each student. (I limit the number of words for this activity to six to keep the examples easy to manage.) Continue the lesson:

I will say a sentence slowly. Then you say it with me as you move a marker into a box for each word we say. <u>Washington was born in February</u>.

Repeat together as markers are moved into five boxes.

Follow Up

Say a few more sentences about a topic and monitor how individuals in your group repeat the sentence slowly and move the markers into the correct number of boxes. Then students can watch you write the words and talk about the spaces between the words.

Using What You Know

During writing time, confer with students about their work as you move about the room. When students say a sentence they want to write, quickly draw boxes on the next blank page and have them push markers into the boxes to match each word. This solidifies for them the number of words in their sentence and where to put spaces as they write.

Use the word box template at right to make individual word boxes for your students.

Sorting Words, Letters, and Numbers

GRADE: K–1	**TIME:** 10–20 minutes

FOCUS: To teach visual discrimination between letters, words, and numbers, and to teach that a group of letters makes up a word (the words *I* and *a* will be in the next lesson)

Materials

* Classroom alphabet and number charts
* Chart paper or whiteboard with a pen
* Copies of word sheet on page 19; enlarge one for teacher modeling
* Copies of three-column sorting mat (on page 156); label columns *Words, Letters (A–Z),* and *Numbers (1, 2, 3)*
* Scissors
* Glue or paste

Sequence

Teach

Begin the lesson like this:

> *Let's look at our alphabet chart and our number line today. We usually use our number line to count and figure out math problems like 4 + 2 = 6. But it can be tricky because sometimes in books we will see letters and numbers together, and they look a lot alike.*

> *Did you know that letters from our ABC chart make words? Let me show you. I can use the c̲ (point to it on your chart), the a̲ (point to it), and the t̲ (point to it on the chart). When I put a group of letters together in a special order, they make a word.*

Write the letters c, a, and t on chart paper or a whiteboard nearby.

C-a-t makes the word cat.

Practice

Begin the guided practice like this:

Today we are going to sort words, letters, and numbers. But we have to really use our eyes because I mixed them all up on this page for you (show them the word sheet from page 19). I want you to check our alphabet chart and number line today to make sure you can tell the difference between letters and numbers. If you see a group of letters together, is that a word, letter, or number? That's right, it will be a word because words can be made from letters.

✳ Pass out the word sheet on page 19 and the three-column sorting mat that you've labeled *Words, Letters (A–Z),* and *Numbers (1, 2, 3)*

✳ Read each box together, commenting on whether each is a word (a group of letters), a letter (refer to it on your classroom ABC chart), or a number (find it on the number line).

✳ As you guide students through the sorting process, have them point out on the sorting mat where they will put each item when they cut it out, under *Words, Letters,* or *Numbers*

✳ Invite students to cut out the boxes and paste each one in the appropriate column on the sorting mat. This activity can be independent or guided depending on your comfort level with how your students understand the concept and the process.

Follow Up

Using some of your favorite counting books that have numerals, have students find words and numbers. I recommend *What Comes in 2's, 3's, and 4's* by Suzanne Aker, (Simon and Schuster Children's Books, 1990).

Using What You Know

In the independent study center, have students cut words, letters, and numbers out of magazines or grocery ads. They can glue them down on the sorting mat used for this lesson.

boy	M	it	s
r	star	7	cat
2	w	is	3
dog	F	stop	the
5	am	mom	8

Learning More About Sorting Words, Letters, and Numbers

GRADE: K–1	**TIME:** 10–20 minutes

FOCUS: To teach that one letter (*I, a*) can be a word but that a word can be long or short; to look at the difference between numbers and letters that look alike (*I and l; 6 and b*)

Materials

* Chart paper or whiteboard and pens
* Copies of word sheet on page 22 for each student; enlarged copy for teacher modeling
* Copies of three-column sorting mat on page 156; label columns *Words, Letters (A–Z),* and *Numbers (1, 2, 3)*, the same way as for the previous lesson
* Scissors
* Glue or paste

Sequence

Teach

Begin the lesson like this:

> *We have learned that letters and numbers are different from words. Remember when we looked at words that had more than one letter?*

Refer to the previous lesson with words like *cat* and *mom.*

> *Well, today is going to be a little bit tricky because I have found two words that have only one letter! Can anyone guess what they are? Yes, there are two letters that when they are all by themselves, with a space on each side, become words: I and a.*

Write an example or two on your chart paper or board: *I have a dog. I see a horse.*

Then continue:

And I have something else to trick you today! If you look closely at some letters, they look very much like numbers. If we don't pay attention when we are reading, we could get them mixed up. Or if we aren't careful when we write, our friends might not be able to figure out what we are trying to say. Look at the number 1 and the letter l (write them on the chart as you note that the number 1 when it is written in books usually has a line at the bottom), and the number 6 and the letter b (add them to your example as you note the very rounded back on the number 6).

But don't worry, we have two ways to beat these tricky letters and numbers and words:

One, when we are reading and writing, we always want to make sense. Getting these mixed up would make the story sound funny, wouldn't it?

Two, we will always look carefully at letters, numbers, and words.

Practice

Pass out the word sheet on page 22 and a three-column sorting mat that you've labeled *Words, Letters (A–7),* and *Numbers (1, 2, 3)* to your large or small group.

Let's do one of each together. Who can find a word in the first row?

Make sure students recognize a can be a letter or a word here. Write the following sentence on chart paper to help them put it in context: We see *a cat.*

Who can find a letter? Who can find a number? (Note: They have to look past the first row to find a number.)

Now you can cut them out and do these by yourselves. I'll come around to check.

Follow Up

During shared reading with a Big Book or guided reading with individual copies of a story, have students locate the words *I* and *a* in the book. Remind them that words usually have more than one letter, but these two are special because when they are by themselves they are a word.

Using What You Know

After hearing children read during guided reading, have them count the number of times they can find *I* and *a* in the story. Make sure they know which are words and which are the letters *i* and *a* within a word.

dad	at	x	a
red	I	4	fun
p	bus	12	no
r	1	pizza	dog
if	6	b	this

Word Learning Word Making Word Sorting: 50 Lessons for Success Scholastic Professional Books

Word Sorting by Word Length

> **GRADE:** K–1 **TIME:** 10–15 minutes
>
> **FOCUS:** To teach students to look carefully at visual details by the size of words, encouraging them to use their compare-and-contrast skills

Materials

* Chart paper or whiteboard and pens
* Copies of two-column sorting mat on page 155; label columns *Short Words/he* and *Long Words/helicopter*
* Copies of word sheet on page 25

Sequence

Teach

Begin the lesson like this:

> *When I am reading, it is important that I look very quickly at a word so that I can keep reading and make sense of the words. One of the things I might notice is how long or short a word is.*

Write out students' names for the group to see, and compare their lengths. Then, pass out the sorting mats and word sheets, and write *he* and *helicopter* on the chart paper or white board. Ask:

> *Which one says helicopter?*

Run your finger under both to check while sounding out slowly.

> *Show me by pointing your thumb . . . which one says helicopter?*

Check for a whole-group response that they are all pointing to the right word on their sorting mat, and help where needed. Repeat quickly with other examples as needed. Choose words with different lengths so students compare their sizes, such as *thunder* and *the*.

Practice

Begin the guided practice like this:

> *Let's read all the words together before we sort them.*

Read through cards from the word sheet on page 25. Continue:.

> *Now cut your words apart and put them in one pile in front of you. Look at a word. Is it long like <u>helicopter</u> or short like <u>he</u>?*

Have each student try one and explain his or her thinking. Then ask:

> *Where would your word go on your sorting mat? Okay, now sort the rest on your own. Look carefully at the size.*

Follow Up

Stress the difference between word lengths, and be sure students understand all the examples are words just like their names.

Using What You Know

* Have students find words in classroom books that are long or short. Then have them record words during independent literacy center activity time.

* Ask students to sort classmates' names written on cards or sentence strips by size. Have them record findings on word mats.

cat	triceratops	see	dog
hippopotamus	no	play	snowman
run	basketball	birthday	fox
the	six	caterpillar	bus
playground	mom	I	Pokéman

Chapter 2

Whole-Word Units

When we teach young children to read, we guide them along a continuum of visual discrimination and word analysis tasks. Research (Neal, 1999) has demonstrated the effectiveness of the following sequence of instruction, in which we teach students to:

* look carefully at whole-word units

* use sub-word parts

* use embedded letters and letter clusters

The lessons in this book follow that continuum. This section looks at whole words, helping students first to understand word units as a whole and then teaching them high-frequency words.

Why We Use High-Frequency Words

I stopped teaching high-frequency words in the 1980s because I connected it to the flash card "kill and drill" techniques I was trying to avoid. When I became a Reading Recovery® teacher, I was brought up short by the power of teaching students a solid core of the most frequently used words. Immediately, I put these words back into my regular classroom instruction, integrating them into authentic reading and writing activities. (See pages 31–32 for ideas on how to do this.) High-frequency words are powerful in writing because knowing them effortlessly leaves "the writer's attention free to work on new challenges" (Clay, 1993). Also, many of the most commonly used words are not spelled as they sound or read as they appear. Repeatedly sounding out common words laboriously and incorrectly, or writing them incorrectly, can habituate responses:

> *There is a danger . . . that spelling* they *as* thay *may become automatic and thus more permanent because* they *is used so frequently in writing. Things that we do the same way over and over become automatic, which means we do them without any conscious attention* (Allington and Cunningham, 1996).

Temporary, or invented, spelling is useful as K–2 students record the sounds they hear in words. In conjunction, knowing a core of high-frequency words makes their writing less tedious and more accurate.

Rebecca Sitton and others have made us aware of the power of these words in writing, but teaching kindergartners and first graders has shown me how they work in reading. When an emergent reader starts reading patterned, predictable stories, the most common words naturally occur repeatedly. These readers are also solidifying the early behavior of pointing to words as they read, monitoring one-to-one correspondence of sound to word. To observers, it appears students have memorized the text and could read the simple pattern with their eyes closed. Then, a flash of insight: A student's finger doesn't match what she's saying, and she notices the mismatch because she knows one of the high-frequency words in the book. I have seen a student reread and self-correct for the first time because of the mismatch between a high-frequency word in print and a spoken word. A solid core of known words helps students to attend to the visual details of print and not just read from the pattern.

Which Word Lists Should We Use?

My comparison of lists of the 20 most common words used for writing (Sitton) and reading (Eeds, 1985) reveals that 15 of the 20 words are the same! See the chart below.

HIGHEST-FREQUENCY WORDS IN WRITING AND READING

Writing Words	Reading Words	Writing Words	Reading Words
1. **the**	**the**	11. **he**	**was**
2. **of**	**and**	12. **for**	she
3. **and**	**a**	13. **was**	**for**
4. **a**	**I**	14. on	**that**
5. **to**	**to**	15. are	**is**
6. **in**	said	16. as	**his**
7. **is**	**you**	17. with	but
8. **you**	**he**	18. **his**	**they**
9. **that**	**it**	19. **they**	my
10. **it**	**in**	20. at	**of**

1998, Judy Lynch. The words in bold appear on both high-frequency reading and writing lists.

Clearly, these should be among the first words students add to their core of familiar words. I have selected words for the lists in this chapter based on the following criteria. They all:

✳ have a high utility in reading

✳ occur most often in the language

✳ are needed most often in writing

The word lists on this page are made up of anchor words for primary students. Teach these words first! When your students can use them in reading and writing, move on to other lists, such as the ones on pages 29 and 30. These words link to reading simple patterned books and the patterned writing common among emergent writers. When known, they "anchor" young readers to the print.

ANCHOR WORDS FOR K–1 STUDENTS

I	a	the
and	to	like
see	can	mom
dad	love	is

100 HIGHEST-FREQUENCY **WRITING** WORDS

1. the	26. or	51. out	76. its
2. of	27. by	52. them	77. who
3. and	28. one	53. then	78. now
4. a	29. had	54. she	79. people
5. to	30. not	55. many	80. my
6. in	31. but	56. some	81. made
7. is	32. what	57. so	82. over
8. you	33. all	58. these	83. did
9. that	34. were	59. would	84. down
10. it	35. when	60. other	85. only
11. he	36. we	61. into	86. way
12. for	37. there	62. has	87. find
13. was	38. can	63. more	88. use
14. on	39. an	64. her	89. may
15. are	40. your	65. two	90. water
16. as	41. which	66. like	91. long
17. with	42. their	67. him	92. little
18. his	43. said	68. see	93. very
19. they	44. if	69. time	94. after
20. at	45. do	70. could	95. words
21. be	46. will	71. no	96. called
22. this	47. each	72. make	97. just
23. from	48. about	73. than	98. where
24. I	49. how	74. first	99. most
25. have	50. up	75. been	100. know

HIGH-FREQUENCY WORDS WITH *NO SPELLING PATTERN*
From the 200 Most Frequent Words For Writing and Reading

(The number reflects their placement on the word list.
The missing numbers represent words with regular spelling patterns.)

1. the	40. your	85. only	149. old
2. of	42. their	90. water	151. great
4. a	43. said	93. very	161. should
5. to	45. do	95. words	165. give
8. you	55. many	98. where	184. something
13. was	56. some	102. through	185. thought
15. are	57. would	115. any	186. both
19. they	60. other	123. another	187. often
23. from	61. into	125. come	194. together
25. have	65. two	126. work	198. world
28. one	70. could	131. does	200. want
32. what	75. been	142. put	
34. were	77. who	144. different	
37. there	79. people	146. again	

These irregular words make up about one-quarter of the most frequent words. The others fit into vowel spelling patterns, (for example, short *a* words: *and, that, can, back*).
Adapted from Dr. John Shefelbine, California State University, Sacramento

How to Teach High-Frequency Words

In the classroom, I teach a few words at a time intensively and continually make links to them in our daily reading, writing, and word-wall activities. This practice builds fluency and flexibility and sets up the expectation that students will read and write these words automatically. By teaching a word briefly in isolation, I target students who need explicit instruction and might not pick up word knowledge incidentally. The most powerful teaching, however, is in authentic reading and writing where high-frequency words naturally occur.

I believe that knowing the exact details of a word makes learning the next word easier because the visual details become important to the student:

- letter order (*no/on*) • letter-sound match • word shape • word length

✔ Expect Success

Learning a core of high frequency words has been most successful for my students when I have high expectations. These words should be, from the first day they are introduced to the class, spelled and read correctly. I set up my students for success by over-teaching the word to begin with, then linking it to our regular reading and writing and making it available on the word wall and table charts. You will often hear me say:

You read that word in this story and you can write it too, right?
Wow! You wrote that word so fast it must have popped out of your brain.
Where can you find out how to spell that word? Where else?

✔ Follow-Up in Your Classroom

The heart of all I teach is the regular practice students engage in as they read and write throughout the day. I look for natural opportunities to prompt students for the words we have learned and praise students who notice these words on their own. Here are just a few of the opportunities that occur daily:

Morning Message

On chart paper, I write a message to my students. I often:

❋ pause at words they know and have them chime in with the spelling.

❋ write the whole message, then invite students to circle high-frequency words.

❋ write the message with the key words missing; I might leave blank spaces to indicate how many letters the word has (_ _ _ = *the*).

Poetry and Songs

Every day while we work in the pocket chart, I:

❋ match high-frequency words on extra cards to those in the chart.

❋ use the poem's pattern to rewrite a line or two, stressing the key words.

Word Walls

I encourage students to refer to our word wall because:

❋ word walls provide children with an immediately accessible dictionary for the most troublesome words.

* words are added gradually, stay in the same spot forever, are listed alphabetically by first letter, and are often made visually distinctive by different colors of paper and by cutting around the configuration.

* through the daily practice of finding, writing, and chanting these words, almost all children learn to read and spell nearly all the words (Cunningham, 1995).

Big Books

As we enjoy old favorites, we can focus on skills allowing students to:

* mark the word with reusable highlighter tape.

* circle high-frequency words with wikki stix, wax-coated yarn that peels off with no residue (both available from 1-800-ART-READ).

Writers' Workshop

As students create their own texts, I expect them to correctly spell all words taught up until that time. I model this using the word wall as a reference during mini-lessons.

Guided Reading

As we read in small groups, I:

* ask students, before reading, to locate one or two important words after they say which letter they would expect to see at the beginning (adapted from Clay, *Reading Recovery Guidebook*, 1993).

* ask students to find high-frequency words on several pages in the text after reading.

* practice writing using the pattern of the book, which should provide repetitions of words we need to cement.

For example:
Text: *Rain on the red car*, from *Rain* by Robert Kalan
Write: *Rain on the red fire truck*, our own innovation of text

Independent Practice In Literacy Centers

Students build the new word with magnetic letters, chalk, pens, clay, or write it in salt, sand, and other such substances.

Building Words With Magnetic Letters

GRADE: K–I	**TIME:** 10–12 minutes

FOCUS: To establish the concept of a word and to introduce working with magnetic letters

Materials

❋ The magnetic letters *i, s* for each student in a small group

❋ A magnetic surface (whiteboard, cookie sheet, or stove burner covers) for each student

❋ Anchor Word list (page 28)

Sequence

Teach

Introduce the concept. Make *is* with magnetic letters. Then say:

> *Here is a word you know: is. Look at the word. Now say it slowly and make it with your letters. Run your finger under it. What's the word? Right, is!*

Move the letters apart: *i s.* Ask students to do the same with their word.

> *Now is it the word is? No? You're right; letters have to be close to be a word. Let's push the letters back together. Do they spell is now? Are you sure? Run your finger under it to check.*

Make sure students check carefully with their fingers and eyes.

Practice

Scramble the letters.

> *Try this: si.*

Ask students to copy with their letters.

> *Does it say is now? Why not? That's right; letters have a special place in words. If we mix them up, they don't make the same word. That's how all words work.*

Follow Up

Repeat the lesson by giving students new letters to check the consistency of letter order in other words they know.

Examples include *the, and, like, see,* the children's names.

Using What You Know

Using a favorite Big Book that has *is* on every page (such as *It Is Weather*), show students how to find the word *is* on each page and how to point under each word to read the simple text. You can also challenge students to find *is* in other Big Books, poems, and guided reading stories you have read as a class.

Teaching High-Frequency Words for Flexibility

GRADE: K–2	**TIME:** 10–15 minutes

FOCUS: To build flexibility with high frequency words, having students construct a new word with a variety of materials on different surfaces.

Materials

* Anchor Word List (page 28) or 100 Word List (page 29)
* Magnetic Letters. Surfaces: magnetic white boards, side of file cabinet, oil drip pan, stove burner covers, cookie sheet
* Chalk. Surfaces: large or individual chalkboards or the sidewalk
* Finger. Surfaces: on top of table, on someone's back, on a chalkboard
* Clean Paintbrush and Water. Surfaces: on a chalkboard, on the sidewalk
* Watercolor Marking Pens. Surfaces: variety of papers
* Salt. Surfaces: baking pan or pizza pan (spray the inside with flat black paint)
* Shaving Cream. Surfaces: tables and desks (great for cleaning!)
* Dry Erase Pens. Surfaces: large whiteboards or individual whiteboards
* Overhead Transparencies and Pens. Surfaces: overhead projector, word cards to trace over
* Crayons. Surfaces: variety of papers

Sequence

Teach

Introduce the lesson like this:

> *When we read and write, I want to make sure that you know each word in every way possible. Good readers can read a word by itself, like on a flashcard,*

and in the middle of a book. Good writers can spell a word when the teacher asks but also when they are writing on their own.

Today we will practice making our words with crayons, chalk, magnetic letters, pens, and many other ways that I will surprise you with soon. You can do this to practice any word from our word wall or words that I give you to practice this week that are new.

Practice

Begin the practice portion of the lesson like this:

Today we will to use color crayons to learn our important words. We can use old or new crayons and any kind of paper. This is called rainbow writing; your words will be as pretty as a rainbow when you are done.

Pass out crayons and paper.

Watch me do the first word _they_. I will choose any color crayon, and as I write the letters, I say them. When we say them while we write them, the word stays in our brain. We say it, hear it, see it, and feel it. We will write each word 5 times so I can use any 5 colors I want.

Model saying the letters as you write it in orange (or any other color).

Now I need to make a tally mark over to the side to remind me I have written _they_ once.

Repeat with 4 more colors, tracing over the word with each color. Make a tally mark for each new color to track how many times you've traced the word.

Now it's your turn to do a word. Don't forget to say the letters softly as you write them and make a tally mark each time.

Walk around checking students' work.

Follow Up

Build in a short, daily practice with different materials and surfaces to cement students' learning of high-frequency words. After teaching the procedure for working in different formats, you can move materials into independent centers for further practice.

Using What You Know

Share all these ideas with parents for home practice in basic letter formation and word review. Writing in shaving cream on the side of the bathtub is especially popular at home.

Teaching High-Frequency Words for Fluency

GRADE: K–2   **TIME:** 10–15 minutes

FOCUS: To teach a key word for reading and writing so it is known fluently and quickly

Materials

* Individual chalkboards or whiteboards
* Erasers (can be old socks or a square of felt)
* Pens or chalk or any materials listed under "Teaching High-Frequency Words for Flexibility" page 35

Sequence

Teach

Begin the lesson like this:

> *Here is our new word: the.*

Point it out and say it.

> *Everybody spell it: <u>the</u>. Now write it. For the <u>t</u>, trace down and then make a cross. Then <u>h</u>. Go down, up and over, down. Then <u>e</u>. Go over, up and around. Now show it to me.*

Ask students to hold up their boards so you can spot check.

Practice

Begin the guided practice like this:

> *I want you to know this word every time you write it or read it, so let's practice. Write it on your boards; then read it aloud.*

Indicating a corner of their board, ask students to write the word; then have them run their fingers under it from left to right.

Now write it again, saying each letter as you write. Then erase it and try it again this time writing it from memory.

See how fast they can write it to build automatic response, and have them write it big, tiny and with their own flourishes. Finally, ask them to say the word again, to make sure they can read it as well as write it

Follow Up

Practice a few minutes daily to review the new word. Also, build in a short practice of former high-frequency words. Over-teaching is okay! During the year, put words you've taught on a word wall that you continually build. Put words taught on student tables for reference in clear plastic holders (inexpensive clear plastic picture frames or restaurant menu holders work well). Also, place words you've reviewed in student writing folders (see "Building Individual Word Walls" on page 41).

Using What You Know

Maintain high expectations: Students should use the words from these lessons in daily reading and writing activities. Remind them of the words every time they see them in a story or try to spell them in their writing.

Memory Matching

GRADE: K–2	**TIME:** 10–15 minutes

FOCUS: To review high-frequency words in a Concentration game-like format

Materials

✴ Pocket chart

✴ Twelve three-by-five-inch index cards with duplicates of each of six words (for example: I, I, the, the, is, is, like, like, can, can, see, see)

✴ Twelve three-by-five-inch index cards to use as covers, numbered 1 through 12

Sequence

Teach

Begin the lesson like this:

Today let's play a memory game. I have made up word cards for some of the words we have been learning. In a minute I'll hide them behind these number cards in the pocket chart. (Show the pocket chart with numbered cards for the game.) First, let's see if you remember them.

Using the three-by-five cards as flash cards, go through the words you will use for the lesson that day.

As I show you the word, don't shout it out. Look carefully and get it in your head. When I point to the whole group, you may read the word together. If I let one of you shout out the word each time, the rest of you won't get a chance to use your own brains.

Show a card; pause; then point to the group to read the word. Continue through the stack of 12 cards.

Now close your eyes so I can hide our words behind the number cards in the pocket chart.

Slip the word cards randomly behind the numbered index cards that are in the pocket chart.

Practice

Choose different students to take turns. Each picks two numbers to see if the words behind the number cards match each other. As you reveal the words behind each pair of number prompts, have the class read them aloud. Ask them if they match each other, and have them shake their heads quietly yes or no. Then hold one card directly over the other to check carefully for a visual and sound match.

When the words don't match, place them back behind the numbers. When words do match, turn the cards over so that only their blank sides are showing. Repeat choosing numbers until all the words have been matched.

Follow Up

Rotate the word cards throughout the year as you teach new high-frequency words that you want to review in a game-like format. Later, when your students are ready, make the words more visually similar: *my, me, mom, the, them, then, there, they* etc.

Using What You Know

Refer to the Memory Match game when students are trying to remember how to spell a word while writing or reading. You can have students play Memory Match in a learning center in pairs.

Credit and thanks to Patty Calabrese, Reading Recovery teacher leader, Robla School District, Sacramento, California

Building Individual Word Walls

GRADE: K–2	TIME: 5–10 minutes

FOCUS: To create a personal word wall for each student in your small group

Materials

* Individual word wall: run page 43 on card stock, one per student

* Pens or pencils

* High-frequency words you have taught, especially those with no spelling patterns (reference page 30)

Some students may need to review words no longer posted on the larger classroom word wall, or you may choose to create personal word walls for students who sit where the bigger board is hard to see. A personal word wall serves as an individual reference for high-frequency words and can be tailored to each student's needs.

Aa	Bb	Cc can	Dd	Ee
Ff	Gg go	Hh	Ii is I	Jj
Kk	Ll	Mm my	Nn	Oo
Pp	Qq	Rr	Ss see	Tt the they
Uu	Vv	Ww	Xx Yy Zz	

Sequence

Teach

Begin the lesson like this:

Sometimes I forget how to spell a word I use often in my writing. I can check my personal word wall so that I spell it right every time. Let me give each of you one and show you how it works. We can use these all the time.

Pass out one to each student.

Practice

Begin the guided practice like this:

> *Here's a word we just did (in guided reading or a writer's workshop mini-lesson) with magnetic letters: was. It can be tricky, so we'll want to look at it carefully. Let me write it quickly on each of your word walls under the letter w. Everybody spell it while I write.*

The whole group chants w-a-s—was—as you write it for each student.

> *This word is tricky because the letters do not match the usual sounds. So we can't sound it out. We must remember what it looks like. Close your eyes and spell it. Were you right? Check your word wall!*

Follow Up

As words are added to the word walls throughout your lessons, be sure to build in one to two minutes of review of words previously taught:

> *Look at t on your word wall. Spell the word they and then say it.*

Students locate the word under *t* on their word wall and chant *t-h-e-y* as they touch under and look at each letter. Then they say the whole word. Another example:

> *I'm looking at the letter m. Spell the word my.*

Students locate it under the m and chant the spelling. Repeat for other words as time allows.

Using What You Know

These personal word walls can be kept in students' writing folders and referenced throughout the day in writing and reading activities.

Do a word hunt as an independent literacy center activity. Give each student a three-inch piece of removable highlighter tape. Ask them to cover the selected word with the tape as they find it in regular classroom materials (Big Books, poems, library books). The tape pulls off easily and can be reused. Students can tally how many times they find the high-frequency word.

Aa	Bb	Cc	Dd	Ee
Ff	Gg	Hh	Ii	Jj
Kk	Ll	Mm	Nn	Oo
Pp	Qq	Rr	Ss	Tt
Uu	Vv	Ww	Xx Yy Zz	

Word Learning Word Making Word Sorting: 50 Lessons for Success   *Scholastic Professional Books*

Word Sorting by High-Frequency Words

GRADE: K–2	**TIME:** 10–15 minutes

FOCUS: To teach students to look carefully at all the letters in a word to match the sounds with the letters

Materials

* High-frequency words
* Copies of word sheet on page 46 (*the, me, to, my*)
* Copies of five-column sorting mat on page 158; label columns *the, to, me, my,* and *No Match*
* Scissors and glue

Sequence

Teach

Begin the lesson like this:

> *When we are reading or writing, it is important that we know how to read and write our high-frequency words. We need to instantly recognize them, using clues like word shape, word length, and letter-sound order.*

> *When it comes to word shape, have you noticed that words can have tall letters or all short letters? Let's look at some class names that are different shapes.*

Write several names on the board and examine their features.

> *Some words are very short, some long. Who has a long name or short name in our class?*

Write them and compare. Then continue.

> *Don't forget the letters have to be in an exact order. Would [student's] name be the same if we mixed it like this [scramble letters]?*

Compare how the sounds don't match when the letters are mixed up.

Practice

Begin the guided practice like this:

> *Now let's read all the word cards before we sort them. Cut apart your word cards and put them in a pile in front of you. Look at the top word; where would it go on your sorting mat? Now sort the rest on your own. Look at the shape, length, and order.*

Monitor students carefully, talking about the visual features.

Follow Up

Using the blank word-card sheet provided on page 154, create new word sorts as you teach new high-frequency words. These make excellent literacy center tasks in a word center. The first sorts should be words that don't look alike (see, *that, was*), but eventually your goal is for students to sort words that are visually similar (*the, they, them, then*).

Using What You Know

Using Big Books and guided reading books, have students locate *to, the, me,* and *my*. Point out the different fonts and that some words may be capitalized, but explain that they still represent the same word.

cat	me	the	to
my	the	man	me
to	my	me	to
mom	the	it	the
time	me	to	my

Word Learning Word Making Word Sorting: 50 Lessons for Success *Scholastic Professional Books*

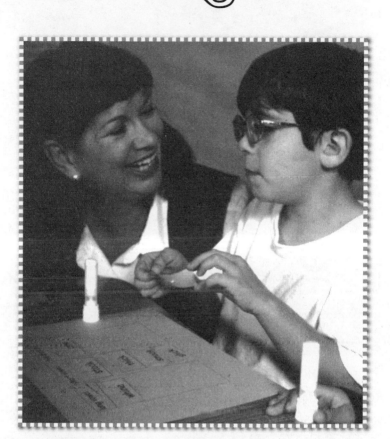

Chapter 3

Learning Word Parts

Working through the lessons and activities in the previous chapters helps students to solidify their understanding of what a word is. As they read simple, predictable stories, they can match spoken words to printed words with their finger, monitoring one-to-one correspondence. They also come to understand many high-frequency words as whole-word units. As they learn more common words, they continue to build fluency and flexibility. But as they progress to less supportive texts, students must start to look more closely at the details of the print in unknown words. This is an opportunity to use their expanding knowledge of letters and sounds in conjunction with the meaning of stories to unlock new words.

Working With Sub-Word Parts

The first use of sub-word parts comes when we draw students' attention to the first letter of a word to confirm what it spells. "Is that *horse* or *pony*?" we ask, and have them look at the first letter to check. We read stories in which the illustrations are less of a match with the print, and this sparks the need to check sub-word parts: initial and final letters, common digraphs (*sh, ch, wh, th*), suffixes like *-ing*, *-ed*, *-er*, and *-s*, and common word patterns (_*at*, _*it*, _*op*). Students move from noticing the beginning of a word to looking across the word at more and more details of the print.

This chapter presents a series of increasingly complex tasks, guiding students to attend to a variety of word parts. An early strategy is to use the beginning letter and picture to confirm a word. Subsequent lessons focus on beginning and ending letter combinations. The last lessons in the chapter introduce the key strategy of "chunking" words. Students learn to recognize a known part (or chunk) and use it to solve a more complex word—the beginning of using analogy to solve words.

The lessons in this chapter, as in all the others, are meant to support the reading and writing lessons already going on in your classroom. The goal here is to have students look more and more closely at the details of a word to solve it in the context of a story. Use the lessons flexibly in conjunction with a shared reading or writing activity, or after a guided reading lesson. All lessons can be done in large or small groups to meet your students' needs.

Using Initial and Final Letters

Although teaching letter names and sounds is not the focus of this book, students must be able to quickly recognize letters before they can use sub-word parts to read new words. We don't want to leave students stuck in the whole-word stage, where they "do not have in place the skills needed for phonological decoding systems; so, they must often read words by sight . . ." (Ehri, 1991). Sight words are important, and we must continue to reinforce and teach these core words. But we must also keep in mind that "children who know how to recognize letters *and* have a small body of words they can read move more easily from the application of letter-sound relationships to the reading of words" (Ehri and Wilce, 1985). In addition, it appears that the more words a child knows and recognizes, the easier it is to learn more words. As children move beyond the early stages of learning to read, we expect an acceleration of their word learning because they have learned *ways of learning words* (Fountas and Pinnell, 1999).

A good way to begin this journey of word-learning, techniques is to focus on sub-word parts: initial and final letters, word endings, such as *-ing* and *-ed*, and simple short vowel patterns, such as *at*, *op*, and *ug*. To begin with, students must recognize the initial letters of words to visually distinguish them from other words. This section includes several lessons dealing with quick recognition of letters and sounds. Further lessons move into letter sorts by initial letters, blends, and digraphs because "word study activities involving blends and digraphs help students see blends and digraphs as one consonant unit" (Bear et al., 1996). Recognizing the beginning consonants as a unit is an essential first step to seeing the vowel pattern or chunk in the rest of the word or syllable. (We will work on vowel patterns and chunks in a later section.) Other lessons in this section provide students with the opportunity to apply their knowledge of initial letters to reading simple stories appropriate for this stage. Predictable books provide lots of support for new readers, but when the pattern changes, students must at least look at the first letter to notice the change. Coaching and prompting students to look carefully at words instead of memorizing text or depending on picture clues helps them begin to attend to print.

> *"Children's first understanding develops through exploring the beginning sounds of words."*   (Bear et al., 1996).

Learning Suffixes

As students gain experience, we want to teach them to look at bigger pieces of visual information. A natural next step is to help them see the larger chunks of letters at the end of words they know, which the lessons in the next section of this chapter cover. If students know the high-frequency word *look*, we can show them how easy it is to look at the end to read *looking*, *looks*, or *looked*. Teaching common suffixes reinforces the important strategy of LOOKING ACROSS THE WORD and will lead them to CHUNKING THE WORD. Using larger groups of letters, such as suffixes, to decode a word is efficient and fosters faster and more fluent reading. I recommend starting by adding suffixes to a word your students already know so all they have to attend to are the endings.

Learning Chunks

The final part of the chapter moves students from attending to larger letter groups when they read a suffix as a whole unit to looking at the vowel pattern or chunk at the end of every word or syllable. Linguists call the vowel pattern that follows the beginning consonants in a word or syllable a *rime*. With students I like to simply call it a chunk. When students use chunk patterns that they know as a way to decode a new word, they are well on their way to reading. Patricia Cunningham confirms that "most researchers believe that by the time children have a fluent first-grade reading level they are using patterns and analogy as their major decoding strategy" (2000).

Unfortunately, my experience shows that too many first, second and even third graders are not efficiently using these effective strategies. Too many approach a new word in panic, thinking it is unique. The lessons in this section walk them through what a chunk is, how to use a chunk chart with a key word and picture for the most common patterns, and how to apply effective chunking strategies. I teach students to look for what they *do know* when approaching a tricky word; this practice encourages them to use analogy. We don't want our primary students staring at an unknown word with no clue about how to take it apart while reading. This chapter helps students to use the tools that efficient word detectives need.

Using the Alphabet Chart

GRADE: K–2   **TIME:** 10–20 minutes

FOCUS: To use a familiar alphabet chart to link sounds to key pictures

Materials

* Alphabet chart (page 53), a copy for each student or small group
* Large letter mask (pattern found on page 54)
* Whiteboard or chart paper and pen

Sequence

Teach

Begin the lesson like this:

Everybody knows the ABC song.

Quickly sing it; they will burst into song!

You know how to sing the song, but let's make sure you also how to say the names of the letters slowly.

Repeat the alphabet without the song, clearly saying the names of the letters as you frame each one on the chart with the large letter mask.

Today we are going to learn to use our alphabet chart to help us read. The pictures on our chart aren't there just to make it pretty. Each picture reminds us of the sound the letter makes in words. Listen as I say the name of the letter, the sound of the letter, and show you a picture of a word that makes that sound: <u>a</u>, /a/, <u>apple</u> . . .

Invite students to repeat after you as you go through the chart. Discuss the pictures and what sound each represents. When making the sounds in isolation, say them as clearly as possible: /r/ should be only that—not /er/; /b/—not /buh/. Differentiating the sound and the name of the letter will take continued practice over many sessions for some children.

Practice

Begin the guided practice like this:

> Let's see how the pictures on our chart can help us to figure out a word when we are reading. If I see a word like this (write bat) and I don't know what it is, I can check the chart to see what sounds the letters make.

If a few kids who might know your sample word are trying to tell everyone the word, ask them to smile at you if they know it but keep it a secret. This allows them to show you how smart they are while you continue to model the strategy for everyone. This lesson is not about reading the word *bat*, but about the strategy of using the pictures on the chart to remember letter sounds. Next, mask the *b* in *bat*.

> Where do I find this on the chart? That's right, with the picture of a bear. The sound at the beginning of the picture word <u>bear</u> helps me to remember the sound of the letter <u>b</u>. Say it after me: <u>bear</u>, /b/.

Repeat this process for the *a* and *t*. Then say:

> Now, I'm going to put those three sounds together quickly so I can hear which word I am saying.

Use whatever word you've chosen to model in a sentence to give meaning to the blending and decoding. For instance, with *bat* I might say:

> <u>At Halloween I saw a flying, black</u> . . . Let's push the sounds together to read our word.

Model by pushing one finger up under each letter as you quickly blend them together going left to right. This draws their eyes to each letter as the group produces the sounds /b/ /a/ /t/.

> What's our word? <u>Bat</u>, that's right! <u>On Halloween I saw a flying, black, b-a-t</u>. Don't forget to use our alphabet chart whenever you need to remember a sound. The pictures help us to do that.

Follow Up

In a writing mini-lesson that day (and on many more days!), model how you can use the same alphabet chart to help with spelling a word. Refer to the pictures as a support when students haven't yet linked letters and sounds.

Using What You Know

Expect students to use the alphabet chart as a tool when reading and writing. Continue to model its use in Big Books, poems, and guided reading and writing lessons.

Alphabet Chart

Aa apple	Bb bear	Cc cat	Dd duck	Ee elephant	Ff fish
Gg goat	Hh horse	Ii igloo	Jj jar	Kk kite	Ll lion
Mm mouse	Nn nest	Oo octopus	Pp pig	Qq queen	Rr rabbit
Ss snail	Tt turtle	Uu umbrella	Vv volcano	Ww watch	Xx x-ray

Yy yo-yo	Zz zebra	ANCHOR WORDS			
		I	a	the	and
		to	like	see	can
		mom	dad	love	is

Letter/Cluster/Word Highlighters. Trace pattern on card stock or lightly colored transparency material. Cut out the center with an exacto knife to provide a small window to show students a letter/cluster/word on the page as they read.

Name Sorting

> **GRADE:** K–2   **TIME:** 15–30 minutes
>
> **FOCUS:** To teach students to look carefully at the first letter of a word by using their names as examples

Materials

❋ First names of students on four-by-six-inch index cards

❋ Pocket chart or other area to hold cards

❋ Alphabet chart (page 53)

❋ Blank sorting boxes (page 154); make one set of class names per student, putting everyone's name in a box (will probably take two pages per student)

❋ Blank paper for sorting on

Sequence

Teach

Begin the lesson like this:

> *Today we are going to look carefully at some very important words—your names!*

Show the index cards with the first names written on them. Put them in the pocket chart in random order. Ask:

> *Who can find their name and tell us which letter it starts with?*

As students come up and find their names, focus on the first letter and where to find it on your class alphabet chart. Note: The following sorting can be done in pairs, teams, or individually. Continue:

> *I noticed that some of you have names that start with the same letter, and some are the only ones whose names use that letter at the beginning. Today, I have put your names on this paper, and we will cut them out. When we have all the names*

cut out, we will see how many start with the same letter. If names start with the same letter, we will glue them down in a group on this second paper. Let's start by cutting out the names and laying them out on the table.

Practice

Begin the guided practice like this:

> Who can find two names that start with the same letter? Raise your hand. Okay, now show us! Class, do the names Sarah and Samantha start with the same letter? Does the first letter look the same? Shake your head yes if you agree and no if you disagree. Good. Where should we glue them down?

Show students how to glue names starting with the same letter in a column on their paper. You may modify this and choose names in order to focus on specific letters. Do as many examples as necessary; then allow for some independent sorting.

Follow Up

In shared reading of Big Books, poetry, or guided reading books, continue to mention beginning letters. Highlight them with wikki stix or highlighter tape. Continue to pay attention to names and the letters they begin with in every context possible.

Using What You Know

In a follow-up center, invite students to write their first name and underline the first letter. Then ask them to cut pictures or words out of magazines and catalogs that feature their letter. They can also work with a partner and sort the name index cards you used to start the lesson.

Matching Pictures and Print

GRADE: K–2	**TIME:** 10–20 minutes

FOCUS: To teach the strategy of cross-checking using the picture (meaning) and the first letter of a word (visual information) to figure out an unknown word (this is an early strategy but lays a foundation for looking at more complex print later)

Materials

* Alphabet chart (page 53)

* Letter mask (pattern on page 54)

* Book(s) with clear examples of needing the print to decode when the picture is vague (I use *My Messy Room* by Mary Packard, Hello Reader, Scholastic Inc., 1993; and *Buzzzz Said the Bee* by Wendy Cheyette Lewison, Hello Reader, Scholastic Inc., 1992)

Sequence

Teach

Begin the lesson like this:

> *Let's look at our alphabet chart again. When I frame each letter* (use mask pattern on page 54), *tell me what you hear.*

On seeing each letter, students should respond with the sound; use the pictures whenever necessary to firm up a connection.

> *Let's see how the pictures on our chart can help us to figure out a word when we are reading. This book is called My Messy Room, and it is about a little girl who likes the mess in her bedroom. In this book, like many others, I can't always figure out the words just from looking at the pictures. Good readers check the picture and then check to see if the letters match.*

Read a few pages to them or with them as they pick up the pattern. Pause on the page that reads *I like toys on my floor* and think aloud:

> *When I check the picture it is hard to tell what the toys are on . . . the rug? the floor? What letter does this last word start with?*

Frame the letter *f* in *floor*.

> *Let's check the picture to remember that sound: /f/ <u>fish</u>. Would you expect <u>rug</u> to start like <u>fish</u>?*

Check the chart and find that *rug* starts like *rabbit*.

> *Let's check to see if it could be <u>floor</u>.*

Help them to discover that *fish* and *floor* start alike.

> *Good. Now we match the picture in the story and the letters on the page when we read. Don't forget to use our alphabet chart whenever you need to remember a sound.*

Practice

Begin the guided practice like this:

> *Let's try to figure out another word in <u>Buzzzz Said the Bee</u>.*

Read the story to enjoy the humor and to pick up the pattern. Pause near the end on the page that reads: *The cow began to weep.* Think out loud again as you use the chart to figure out *weep*. Could it be *cry*? or *weep*? Use the chart to confirm the beginning sound of each word since both make sense in the story and in the picture.

Follow Up

In small-group reading lessons review how to use the chart. Give children small sticky notes and tell them to mark a word that they figured out on their own by using the chart. After reading, call on each child to show her word and verbalize how she used the chart.

Using What You Know

Expect students to use the alphabet chart during reading and writing until they have internalized the process of figuring out words by looking at beginning letters. The chart should be reproduced for each student.

Word Matching With Capital and Lower-Case Letters

> **GRADE:** K–1   **TIME:** 10–15 minutes
>
> **FOCUS:** To make sure students can quickly identify words (whether they start with a capital or a lower-case letter)

Materials

* Copies of 2-column sorting mat for each student (page 155); label columns *Words Beginning with Upper Case Letters* and *Words Beginning with Lower Case Letters*
* Copies of word sheet on page 61 for each student
* Alphabet chart (page 53)
* Writing space for demonstration (chart, whiteboard, overhead projector)

Sequence

Teach

Begin the lesson like this:

> *I have noticed that sometimes you know a word when it is written in lower-case, or small, letters. But when you see the same word written with a capital for the first letter, you act like it is a new word. What is this word?*

Write the word *can* or another word they know.

> *And what is this word?*

Write the word *Can* to compare.

> *That's right, both are the word <u>can</u>. It doesn't matter whether the first letter is a capital or not; it is spelled with the same letters that make the same sound . . . so it is the same word. Now tell me this word.*

Write the word *it* for them to read.

> *Watch out now, I am going to try to trick your eyes. What is this?*

59

Write *It*.

> *You have to be very careful with the capital letter I. When it is by itself, it is the word I and is used when you are talking about yourself.*

Give a few examples.

> *But when it is with other letters, it is part of that word and can have the sound of I or the sound of /i/ like in igloo.*

You can also give a few examples from classroom Big Books or guided reading books where the capital *I* is printed like the letter *l*, which makes it even harder to read.

Practice

Begin the guided practice like this:

> *I have some words here that start with the same letter, but you have to look for the capital and lower-case letters to match them. Sometimes the capital and lower case look very much alike.*

Refer to the words *Can* and *can* that you used before.

> *When they're like this, they're easier to read. But many times the capital and lower case of the same letter don't look the same. We may have to check our alphabet chart to be sure. Which letters on our alphabet chart have capitals and lower-case letters that don't look alike?*

Refer to the alphabet chart page 53. Students should generate these quickly and we need to always comment: *But they are the same letter and make the same sound, /____/.* Then pass out the word sheets and have students point to the words as you read them aloud together.

> *Now cut them out, mix them up, and look for the words that match. Glue them down after I have checked them.*

Follow Up

If students need more practice, you can repeat the matching exercise with words whose initial letters look different in capital and lower case; see the chart at right. Words to use: *Run/run, And/and, Hat/hat, Dog/dog, Like/like, It/it.*

Alphabet Letters Where Capital and Lower Case Don't Match							
Aa	Bb	Dd	Ee	Ff	Gg	Hh	Ii
Jj	Kk	Ll	Mm	Nn	Qq	Rr	Tt

Letters That Match/Look the Same				
Cc	Oo	Pp	Ss	Uu
Vv	Ww	Xx	Yy	Zz

Cat	no	is	The
the	you	Ball	go
Is	cat	No	Mom
Go	mom	You	ball

Word Sorting by Initial Letters

> **GRADE:** K–1   **TIME:** 10–15 minutes
>
> **FOCUS:** To focus on the visual details of the beginning of words

Materials

✳ Copies of word sheet (page 64) for sorting words by initial letters: *m, s, f, b,* (notice *zoo* and *the* are added for the *No Match* category)

✳ Copies of 5-column sorting mat (page 158); label columns *m, s, f, b,* and *No Match*

✳ Wikki stix, or highlighter tape (see page 159 for resources)

Sequence

Teach

Begin the lesson like this:

> *To become a better reader, I have to look not just at whole words but at parts of words. Today we will look at the first letters in words and match them to other words that start with the same letter. Here are some words.*

Write: sew, *farm*, boy, *mom* on the board, overhead, or chart paper.

> *This word is <u>sew</u> (point it out to the group). Show me by pointing your thumbs: where is the beginning of the word, the very first letter?*

Check for a whole group response that they are all pointing to the left, helping where needed.

> *What is the first letter in <u>sew</u>?* (Frame their response to show the s with a wikki stix or highlighter tape.) *Good, we'll be looking for other words that start like <u>sew</u> today.*

Repeat quickly with *farm, boy,* and *mom* while stressing that students look at the beginning of the word and name the initial letters.

Practice

Continue the lesson like this:

> *Let's read all the words together before we sort them. (Read them aloud as a class.) Now read the words on your own.*

Check that they can read the words.

> *Now cut your words apart and put them in one pile in front of you. Look at a word. Does it start like sew, farm, boy, mom or is there no match?*

Have each student try one and explain his or her thinking.

> *Now sort the rest on your own, looking carefully at the beginning of the word.*

Follow Up

Repeat the lessons with other beginning letters. Bear et al. (1996) suggest words with the following beginning consonants: *b, m, r, s; t, g, n, p; c, h, f, d; l, k, j, w; y, z, v, q.* See the chart at right for suggested words. As you do more lessons, check that students are looking carefully at initial letters and noticing small details that make those letters unique in shape, size, and direction.

Using What You Know

Have students find words that begin with *s, f, b, m* in classroom Big Books, poems, or a current guided reading story. Frame the words with wikki stix. This can be an independent literacy center activity.

Future Sorting by:
INITIAL LETTERS

Use the blank sorting boxes (page 154) to create new word sorts using initial letters. These word sorts are based on letters that are grouped by their frequency and are visually and phonetically distinct (Bear et al. 1996). Be sure to also include words that do not go into any category and will be placed under "No Match."

b	m	r	s
be	mom	run	so
boy	me	red	see
by	my	rat	said

t	g	n	p
to	go	no	play
ten	gas	nine	put
tell	girl	not	pass

c	h	f	d
cat	hat	fat	dog
cow	how	fun	do
cut	hut	for	dad

l	k	j	w
like	kit	jump	way
love	king	jet	we
look	kiss	just	will

y	z	v	qu
yes	zoo	vase	queen
yo-yo	zebra	vest	quilt
yellow	zigzag	van	quiet

Bear et al., *Words Their Way: Word Study for Phonics, Vocabulary, and Spelling Instruction,* Merrill, Upper Saddle River, NJ, 1996, p. 153-4.

man	fish	said	no
ball	so	boat	mop
fun	zoo	fire	sun
bee	fly	mom	box
me	the	dog	see

Word Learning Word Making Word Sorting: 50 Lessons for Success *Scholastic Professional Books*

mouse	nest	octopus
S s	**T t**	**U u**
snail	turtle	umbrella
Y y	**Z z**	I
		to
yo-yo	zebra	mom

from *Word Learning, Word Making, Word Sorting: 50 Lessons for Success* by Judy Lynch, Scholastic Professional Books, 2002
Illustrations by Yvette Banek

 pig

 queen

 rabbit

V v
 volcano

W w
 watch

X x
 x-ray

ANCHOR WORDS

a	the	and
like	see	can
dad	love	is

Word Making With Initial Letters

GRADE: K–2	**TIME:** 10–20 minutes

FOCUS: To listen for the first sound in a dictated word and match it to letters, with an emphasis on changing the first sound or letter.

Materials

* Paper letters (see page 66) or magnetic letters: *a, c, f, n, r, t* (one set per student)
* Alphabet chart, page 53
* Pocket chart
* Three-by-five-inch index cards with the words *at, cat, fat, rat, ran, fan, can*

Sequence

Teach

Begin the lesson like this:

> *We have been reading lots of books lately and noticing that we must check more than the picture to figure out a word.*

Refer to a recent Big Book or guided reading lesson where the picture isn't an exact match for the text to be read.

> *Today we will make some words where the letters change at the beginning and even sometimes at the end. Are you ready to listen carefully and look closely? What is the name of this letter?*

Show the *a.*

> *What do you <u>hear</u> when you see it?*

This prompts them to say the sound of the letter *a.* Now give each student an *a,* prompting them to say its sound each time you hand someone a letter. Pass out the remaining letters in the same way.

Practice

Begin the guided practice like this:

Take two letters and make <u>at</u>. <u>We are at school.</u> at. Run your finger under it as you say it slowly.

Monitor that students match their fingers and eyes to the letters as they slowly say the word. Read the word card together for *at* as you put the index card into the pocket chart.

Add one letter and make <u>cat</u>. <u>I have a gray cat.</u> cat.

Read it together and watch as students point to the letters; then add the word card for *cat* to the pocket chart.

Change one letter and make <u>fat</u>. <u>The mouse has fat cheeks.</u> fat. Where do you hear the change? Does it sound like /f/ <u>fish</u>?

Refer to the alphabet chart whenever needed to make connections. Read and add the word card to the pocket chart for each word, and comment on the changes at the beginning of the words.

Change one letter and make <u>rat</u>. <u>I have a pet rat.</u> rat.

Change one letter and make <u>ran</u>. <u>I ran fast at recess.</u> ran. Careful, where do you hear the change? What letter do you need to change?

Change one letter and make <u>fan</u>. Listen to where you hear the change: <u>fan</u>. <u>A fan keeps me cool.</u> fan.

Finally, Change one letter and make <u>can</u>. <u>I can make lots of words today.</u> can.

Follow Up

At an independent center, have the students write the words they made during the lesson on the blank word boxes on page 154, referring to the words in the pocket chart. Have students cut out the words and sort them by beginning letters.

Using What You Know

In Big Books and guided reading stories, point out words that begin with the letters *a, c, f, n, r,* and *t* and refer to the words made in this lesson.

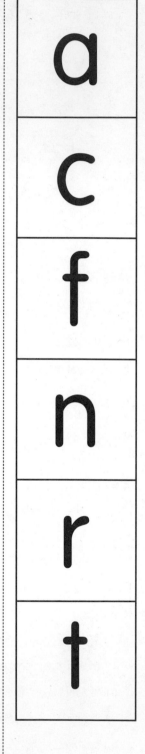

Word Sorting With Blends

GRADE: 1–2	TIME: 10–20 minutes

FOCUS: To teach students to recognize letter blends

Materials

* Copies of the four-column sorting mat on page 157; label columns *f, fl, fr,* and *No Match*
* Copies of the word sheet on page 69
* Glue
* Chart paper or whiteboard and pens

Sequence

Teach

Begin the lesson like this:

You have gotten very good at looking at the first letter of a word in a book you are reading. This is very important, but it is only the beginning of what good readers need to know. From now on, we are going to be looking across a word to be sure what it is. For example, I could be reading about a boy and his mom going to buy food. I might come to this sentence:

Write: *They went in the shop.* Read together up to *shop* and pause.

If I looked only at the first letter in this last word I might guess that it says <u>store</u>. *But good readers don't guess! A word has to make sense and match all the letters. Let's look at all the letters. Can this say* <u>store</u>?

Run your finger under the word *store* as the class slowly says it with you.

Does it match all the letters? No? Good. You're using your eyes. The word begins with /sh/. Let's see if it matches the sounds and letters in <u>shop</u>. *Yes, it does! So the big lesson we are learning today is to* LOOK ACROSS THE WHOLE WORD. *Let's practice that with some sorting of words that may or may not begin alike.*

Practice

Pass out the word sheet and the sorting mat. Read through the words together to make sure students understand they are looking at more than the first letter *f*; they are also sorting for words that begin with *fl* and *fr* or don't match. Then ask students to glue down word cards in the appropriate column on the mat, helping them as needed.

Follow Up

In an independent center, invite students to find more words that start with *f*, *fl*, or *fr* in magazines and newspapers. Students can write the words on the sorting mat they used for the above lesson. Alternatively, you can provide extra copies of the sorting mat in the center and ask students to cut out the words and glue them on the sorting mat.

Using What You Know

Remind students to look at more than the first letter to confirm that *all* the letters match the sounds they expect from the word. Review this in shared and guided reading lessons.

Word Categories for Future Sorting: INITIAL LETTERS—ADVANCED

Use the blank sorting boxes on page 154 to create new word sorts using initial letters, blends, and digraphs. The word sorting should become more visually challenging, as your K-2 students are ready. Be sure to also include words that do not go into any category and will be placed under "No Match."

st	s	t
stop	sat	top
start	sap	tap
stun	sun	tin
stay	say	tray

sp	s	p
spot	sky	pass
spin	slid	put
spill	sill	pill
spell	sell	pan

st	sp	sk	sm
stop	spot	skirt	small
step	sport	sky	smell
stick	spin	skin	smart

sl	sn	sc	sw
slip	snip	scar	swim
slim	snob	scab	swell
slap	snap	school	swan

gl	pl	bl	cl
glue	plan	black	clap
glass	play	blue	cliff
glad	plug	blast	class

sh	s	h
shop	sock	hop
shut	sun	hut
she	see	he
ship	sip	hip

ch	c	h
chin	cat	hen
chest	crest	his
check	can	hand
child	cap	hat

sh	ch	th
shell	church	the
shall	chirp	they
shack	chill	that
shop	chip	this

bl	br	gl	gr
blow	brown	glad	grand
black	bring	glum	gray
blue	brush	glass	grab

cl	cr	fl	fr
club	crack	flash	from
clay	crop	fly	fry
clap	cross	flap	friend

gr	tr	dr	pr
gray	try	dry	pry
grip	trip	drip	print
grow	trap	drop	prop

wh	qu	tw	sw
why	quit	twin	swim
what	queen	twig	swell
where	quilt	twenty	swan

Adapted from suggested sequence by Bear et al., *Words Their Way: Word Study for Phonics, Vocabulary, and Spelling Instruction*, Merrill, Upper Saddle River, NJ, 1996, p. 192.

fun	lit	flat	for
free	after	front	run
off	fat	flower	like
fly	Friday	frost	flip
rat	food	fling	from

Final Endings: Simple Word Making

> **GRADE:** 1–2   **TIME:** 10–20 minutes
>
> **FOCUS:** To learn to look across words and focus on endings

Materials

* Magnetic surface and magnetic letters: *c, c, a, a, t, n, p, b*
* Paper letters (see page 71) or magnetic letters: *a, g, h, m, r, s, t*
* Three-by-five-inch index cards with the words *hat, ham, has, hag, rag, rat, ram*
* Pocket chart
* Alphabet chart, page 53

Sequence

Teach

Begin the lesson like this:

> *We are learning how important it is to LOOK ACROSS A WORD when we are reading. To help us practice this important strategy, today we will look at words that begin the same but look different at the end. Here is a word you know: <u>cat</u>.*

Make *cat* with magnetic letters; then mix up the letters and ask a student to rebuild the word.

> *I'll make the same one: <u>cat</u>.*

Make *cat* again directly under the student's word. Demonstrate that you can make a new word by simply changing the final letter of a word; leave the top version of *cat* and change the bottom one to make *can, cap,* and *cab*.

As you make each word, lead students in reading across it to the end to discover each new word; practice reading the words several times.

Practice

Begin the guided practice like this:

> *Now you will get your own letters for word making; be careful to read all the way to the end to make sure your word looks right and matches the word I say.*
>
> *Take three letters and make <u>hat</u>. <u>I wore a hat today</u>. <u>hat</u>.*

Make sure students run their finger under each letter and blend the sounds at the end to check.

> *Change one letter and make <u>ham</u>. <u>We had a ham sandwich</u>. <u>ham</u>. Where did you hear the change? Beginning, middle, or end?*
>
> *Now let's change one letter and make has. <u>He has a nice sister</u>. <u>has</u>.*
>
> *Let's change another letter to make <u>hag</u>. <u>A hag is like an old witch</u>. <u>hag</u>.*
>
> *What if we change a letter to make <u>rag</u>. <u>We used a rag to clean</u>. <u>rag</u>. Did I trick you? Where did you hear the change? What letter says /r/ like in <u>rabbit</u>?*
>
> *Let's change another letter to make <u>rat</u>. <u>We had a pet rat</u>. <u>rat</u>.*
>
> *Finally, let's change a letter to make <u>ram</u>. <u>Please don't ram my car with yours</u>. <u>ram</u>.*
>
> *How did you do? Did you check all the way across each word? Good, that's what readers do!*

Follow Up

In an independent center, have students write the words from this lesson (*hat, ham, has, hag, rag, rat, ram*) on the blank word sheet on page 154. Ask students to cut out the words and sort by ending letters.

Using What You Know

In shared and guided reading lessons, look for every opportunity to point out the necessity of looking across a word. Encourage students to share words that they solved by using this strategy.

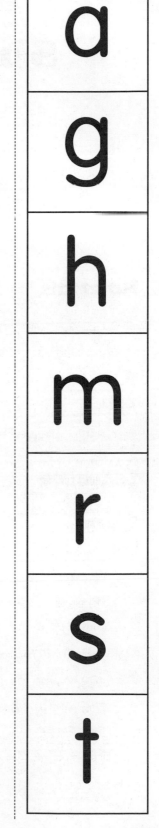

Final Endings: Simple Word Sorting

GRADE: 1–2	**TIME:** 10–20 minutes
FOCUS:	To learn to look across a word and focus on the details at the end

Materials

* Copies of the five-column sorting mat on page 158; label columns *loft, loss, lock, lost,* and *No Match*
* Copies of the word sheet on page 74
* Glue
* Chart paper or whiteboard and pens

Sequence

Teach

Begin the lesson like this:

> *Today we are going to do a word sort that will remind us how important it is to LOOK ACROSS A WORD when we are reading. Here are some words that look the same at the beginning.*

Write *th, th, th,* and *th* on chart paper or a whiteboard, going down in a column.

> *Just from looking at the beginning of these words, can you tell which one says the, which one says then, which one says them, and which one says they? No, of course not! But sometimes people only look at the beginning. They see the t and the h and guess the rest of the word. Do we guess when we read? No way! Now let's put up the rest of the letters and see what happens when we LOOK ACROSS A WORD and think what would make sense in a sentence.*

Add the ending letters to make each word; then use each in a sentence. Pause at the word, allowing everyone to read across it:

them	"Give it to . . . <u>them</u>."
the	"I like . . . <u>the</u> cat."
they	"What do . . . <u>they</u> want?"
then	"What will we do . . . <u>then</u>?"

Practice

Begin the guided practice like this:

Let's sort some words that look the same at the beginning so that we have to LOOK ACROSS THE WORD to see the ending.

Pass out a copy of the word sheet and sorting mat to each student. Make sure everyone knows what to sort for: *loft, loss, lock,* and *lost.* All others go under *No Match.*

Let's read the words together. Be sure to LOOK ACROSS THE WORD.

Explain what the words mean or use them in a sentence as you go through them.

Cut out the words and sort them on your sorting mat. Have a friend check that you have them in the right place before you glue them down.

Monitor as they work independently.

Follow Up

On the blank word sheet on page 154, write in: *the, they, then, them, that, there,* and *this* for students to read and sort independently in a center on a 7-column sorting mat labeled with the words.

Using What You Know

Continue to prompt students during guided reading to decode unknown words by what makes sense and looks right, reminding them to read across the words.

lost	long	loft	lock
loss	lock	loot	lost
look	lost	loss	loft
lock	loft	lock	loss
lost	loss	loft	loop

Word Learning Word Making Word Sorting: 50 Lessons for Success *Scholastic Professional Books*

Adding and Finding Endings

> **GRADE:** 1–2   **TIME:** 15–20 minutes
>
> **FOCUS:** To learn to read words with common suffixes

Materials

* Magnetic surface (stove burner cover or small cookie sheet)
* Magnetic letters: *j, u, m, p, i, n, g, e, d, r, s*
* Chart paper or whiteboard and pens
* Book that has words with suffixes as examples (I am using *Have You Seen Birds?*, by Joanne Oppenheim, Scholastic Inc., 1986, in the following lesson; see page 77)

Sequence

Teach

Begin the lesson like this:

Here is a word you all know.

Make *jump* with magnetic letters.

Let's do "mix-it, fix-it" to make sure.

Scramble the letters as you say "mix-it."

Who can "fix-it"?

Ask a student to come up and put the word in order.

Let's check; say the letters.

Students name the letters as you pull them down.

Okay, let's make sure the sounds match.

Students say the sounds as you push the letters back up.

Great. You do know the word jump. Let me show you how we can make more words from a basic word like this.

Bring -*ing* down to the right of *jump*.

> *If I add /ing/ to* jump *I have* jumping. *Watch me run my finger under it to be sure.*

Have students join with you in saying *jumping*.

> *I'll write it here on our chart under the basic word* jump.

Continue by making *jumped, jumper,* and *jumps*. Each time you assemble a word, read it together and write it on the chart vertically under the word *jump*. Talk about what each word means or use it in a sentence so that the words are familiar.

> *What is the same about each word?*

Get them to understand that they all start with *jump*.

> *Who would like to come up and underline the part* jump *while we read each word?*

Let various students underline jump in each word as the group reads it.

> *It is easy to read long words when we look for the part we know at the beginning and then just read the ending*

Practice

Begin the guided practice like this:

> *Let's look for more words with these endings:* ing, ed, er, s.

Pass out copies of a page from *Have You Seen Birds* (page 77; or use another book your students know) and ask students to work in pairs or small groups to discover more words with these common suffixes. Have them record the words and share their findings with the group.

Follow Up

In an independent center, invite students to find words with these same endings in Big Books or guided reading books with which they're already familiar. Record in a simple Word Book you make at the beginning of the year. (Simply staple a construction paper cover around blank pages of lined paper; see page 152 for a cover sheet.)

Using What You Know

Continue during regular reading to praise students who notice these suffixes, and talk about how to read words with them. Have students record words with suffixes on sticky notes as they read, and then ask them to share their findings.

Or early summer garden birds?
Nesting snugly in the shrubs,
pulling worms and snapping grubs,
finding food to feed the brood,
drinking, singing,
splashing, swinging.
Have you seen birds?

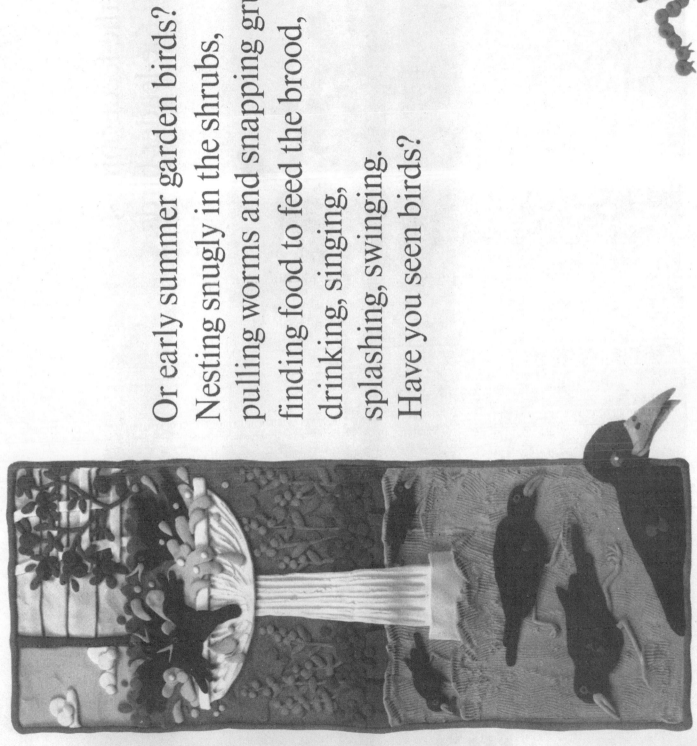

Word Making With Suffixes

GRADE: 1–2	**TIME:** 15–20 minutes
FOCUS: To learn to make new words with suffixes from basic words	

Materials

* Paper letters (page 79): set of *a, e, i, d, g, l, n, p, s, s, t, y* for each student
* Chart paper or whiteboard and pens
* Pocket chart
* Three-by-five-inch index cards with these words: *play, plays, playing, played, stay, stays, staying, stayed*

Sequence

Teach

Begin the lesson like this:

We have been learning to read longer words because we know endings like -s, -ed, and -ing. Remember jump, jumps, jumped, jumping?

Write the words vertically so students can see how *jump* lines up and the suffixes stand out at the end.

We can also do that with another word you know: look.

Write *look, looks, looked,* and *looking* vertically to emphasize the base word and endings.

Today we are going to do word making, and you will have a chance to make these endings on your own.

Pass out a set of paper letters to each student.

Practice

Begin the guided practice like this:

Take four letters and make play. I play tetherball. play.

Help as needed with the *ay* pattern. Explain that it takes two letters to make this one sound.

> Add one letter to make <u>plays</u>. <u>Josh plays tetherball</u>. <u>plays</u>.

> Now, let's change the end of <u>play</u>. Take three new letters and make <u>playing</u>. <u>Josh is playing tetherball right now</u>. <u>playing</u>.

> Let's change the end of <u>play</u> again. Use only two letters to make <u>played</u>. <u>Josh played tetherball yesterday</u>. <u>played</u>.

Depending on the level of your group, you might point out that the word *play* changes its ending based on *who* is playing (I *play*, Josh *plays*) and *when* they do it (*play, playing, played*).

> Watch out. Now I might trick you! Look at <u>played</u>; then take two new letters, and change it to <u>stayed</u>. <u>Sarah stayed at my house</u>. <u>stayed</u>.

> Now use only five letters to make <u>stays</u>. <u>Sarah stays at my house a lot</u>. <u>stays</u>.

> Let's completely change the ending by using three new letters to make <u>staying</u>. <u>Sarah is staying at my house right now</u>. <u>staying</u>.

> Great work. Now I want you to look for other words with -<u>s</u>, -<u>ed</u>, and -<u>ing</u> at the end when you read. Already you know you can read a base word like <u>play</u> and do the ending quickly

Follow Up

Have students write the words you have made in the lesson on a blank word sheet (page 154). They can then cut the words out and sort by base words, -s endings, -ed endings, and -ing endings. They can also do *jump* and *look* words for extra credit. Have them sort on a 3-column sorting mat (page 156) with headings labeled -*s*, -*ed*, and -*ing*.

Using What You Know

During independent reading times, give each student a piece of highlighter tape. Invite students to highlight words in their books with the suffixes -*s*, -*ed*, and -*ing* and record them in their Word Books. The highlighter tape peels off and can be reused.

a	e	i	d	g	l
n	p	s	s	t	y

Word Sorting With Suffixes

GRADE: 1–2   **TIME:** 10–20 minutes

FOCUS: To learn to sort and read words with common endings

Materials

✷ Copies of word sheet on page 82

✷ Copies of four-column sorting mat on page 157; label columns *-ing,- s, -ed,* and *No Match*

✷ Highlighter tape (reusable; see page 159) or highlighter pens

✷ Scissors and glue or paste

Sequence

Teach

Begin the lesson like this:

> *Today before we do our word sorting, I want to show you a way to quickly read words with endings like –ing, –ed, and -s. You know that one of our important strategies is to LOOK ACROSS A WORD. If you don't know the word, but notice an ending that you do know, it will help you to read the word.*

Pass out the word sheet and highlighter tape or pens.

> *With your highlighter tape or pen, find a word and highlight the ending. Who can show us how to read the beginning or base word and then quickly add the ending you have highlighted?*

Invite several students to share examples of *-s, -ed,* and *-ing* endings. Students who have trouble with the sorting later can highlight the suffixes on their word cards for increased support.

> *Now when you are reading a book, you can't always highlight the ending. But you can cover up the ending with your right thumb, read the base word, and quickly add the ending as you uncover it.*

Model this and have them practice the strategy with a few more words.

Practice

Begin the guided practice like this:

> Let's read our words together before you begin to sort. When we read words that have -ed at the ending, I want to remind you that there are three possible sounds for -ed at the end of a word: /t/ as in jumped; /d/ as in yelled; /ed/ as in landed.

Write the three examples and practice each with the group.

> Your ear will tell you which one sounds like the real word. For example: /yell/-/t/, /yell/-/ed/, or /yell/-/d/. See what I mean?

Refer to these three examples as you come to -ed words on the sorting sheet.

> Now cut your words out, sort by endings, and glue them down on your sorting mat.

Follow Up

Have students add to their Word Books as they do independent reading. Teach them to use the highlighter pens responsibly, and let them highlight the suffixes in their Word Books as they record new words.

Using What You Know

Look for every opportunity for students to read longer words with these and other suffixes (-er, -est, -ly). Prompt them to read the base word, covering up the ending if needed with their right thumb, and then quickly add the ending as a unit.

seeing	ships	joked	jumping
boys	yelled	talking	called
fishing	friend	looked	laying
crash	bumps	playing	girls
snowed	sheep	cows	stopped

Word Learning Word Making Word Sorting: 50 Lessons for Success   *Scholastic Professional Books*

Dictation: Clap the Syllables

> **GRADE:** 1–2   **TIME:** 15–20 minutes
>
> **FOCUS:** To use what students know about suffixes in reading to spell words for writing

Materials

* Paper
* Pencils
* Chart paper or whiteboard and pens
* Highlighter pens

Sequence

Teach

Begin the lesson like this:

> We have been learning that many base words can be changed with endings like *-ing*, *-ed*, *-er*, and *-s*. This has helped us in reading words in books, but it can also help with spelling these words in our writing.

> Let's start with a word you know: *cook*. How do you spell *cook*? *I like to cook spaghetti*. (Write the word as they spell it.) Now you write it.

> I want to change it now to *cooking*. *I am cooking spaghetti*. *cooking*. To make this easier to spell, I can break it into syllables—the parts we break it into when we say *cooking*. Say *cooking* and clap it with me so we can hear the parts: *cook-ing*. How many parts do you hear? What do you hear first in *cook-ing*? I can write that first (model writing the first syllable cook). Now say *cook-ing* again; what do you hear at the end that is easy to spell and add to the word? After you write *cooking*, use your highlighter pen to underline the ending *ing*.

Continue clapping the syllables and writing *cook-ed* (watch out for how the /t/ sound is spelled), and *cook-er*. The students should clap, write the base word, repeat the word, and add the suffix. You can also do *cooks*, which has only one syllable but has an easily recognizable sound added. Highlight the endings by underlining as you go.

Practice

Begin the guided practice like this:

I will give you the base word to spell, and then I will give you other forms of the word to write. If the word has more than one syllable or part, it helps to clap the parts and spell the beginning first, and then add the ending. After you write the words, highlight the ending.

Dictation words to use in sentences

bump	bumps	bumping	bumper	bumped
pack	packs	packing	packer	packed
keep	keeps	keeping	keeper	

Follow Up

Using the same instructions as above, give students these words for further practice: *melt, melts, melting, melted; stand, stands, standing; rent, rents, renter, rented, renting.*

Using What You Know

Continue to link what students know in reading to what they can spell in writing. Remind them of this often in guided reading or shared writing. Expect them to clap multi-syllabic words for spelling in independent writing activities.

Word Sorting for -ed Patterns

> **GRADE:** 1–2   **TIME:** 10–20 minutes
>
> **FOCUS:** To recognize the -ed ending and be flexible when pronouncing its three sounds

Materials

* Copies of word sheet on page 87
* Copies of four-column sorting mat on page 158; label $\dfrac{jumped}{t}$, $\dfrac{yelled}{d}$, $\dfrac{landed}{ed}$ and *No Match*
* Four-by-six-inch word cards labeled *jumped /t/, yelled/d/,* and *landed /ed/*
* Scissors and glue or paste

Sequence

Teach

Begin the lesson like this:

> *We have just been learning that when we LOOK ACROSS A WORD we might know an ending that will help us to read the base word. When we have -ed at the end of a word, however, we must remember there are three sounds for the -ed. That means we might have to try more than one sound to solve the word. Who remembers one or more of the sounds of -ed?*

Allow students to recall the three sounds, prompting as needed. Bring out the three word cards with the key words to remember: *jumped /t/, yelled /d/, landed /ed/.*

> *Remember to use your ears today, as well as your brain. If you say a word with the wrong -ed sound at the end, it won't make sense or it will sound like the word but funny.*

Practice

Pass out words for sorting and the mat for recording them.

Let's read our words for sorting. Some of them we might have to read more than once to get the right sound at the end.

This process may take some time as you sort out the sounds with students. You can judge your group; some may be ready to cut out their words and sort independently, while others may need to continue with your coaching and do it as a group activity.

Follow Up

In an independent center, give students these extra words to read and record in pencil on their sorting mat under /t/ /d/ and /ed/: *crashed, slowed, waited, helped, backed, thanked, patted, acted, lifted, talked,* and *cooled.*

Using What You Know

After a reading lesson, have students look for words in the story that end with *-ed.* As a group, make a list, then sort them based on the three ending sounds.

peeled	nested	raked	rowed
called	rotted	smelled	said
batted	looked	pinched	wished
jammed	skipped	friend	wanted
stopped	played	packed	snowed

Vowel Song

> **GRADE:** 1–2   **TIME:** 10–20 minutes, as a daily activity, until it is learned
>
> **FOCUS:** To learn the difference between vowels and consonants in names so that students can later identify vowel patterns in words

Materials

* Chart paper or whiteboard
* Two colors of pens
* Alphabet chart (page 53)
* Highlighter tape or wikki stix (see page 159)

Sequence

Teach

Begin the lesson like this:

> *Today I am going to teach you a song about your names and the letters in them. You will probably know the tune because we have sung "Bingo" before.*

If needed, go over the song: "There was a farmer had a dog and Bingo was his name-o. B-I-N-G-O, B-I-N-G-O, B-I-N-G-O, and Bingo was his name-o."

> *The new words to this song teach us the alphabet letters that are called vowels. Let's look at our alphabet chart and find the vowels.*

Refer to your alphabet chart and identify *a, e, i, o, u, and sometimes y.* It is helpful to highlight them with highlighter tape or a wikki stix ring.

Listen carefully. Here is our new song*: (substitute your name and a new student name daily)

Mrs. Lynch had a student and Sarah was her name-o.
A-E-I-O-U, A-E-I-O-U, A-E-I-O-U,
and Sarah was her name-o

Encourage them to sing along while Sarah stands up and helps you point to the vowels on your alphabet chart while they sing them.

Practice

Begin the guided practice like this:

Now let's write Sarah's name and see which of the letters are the vowels and which are letters called consonants.

Write *Sarah* for all to see with a dark pen.

Think about which letters in her name are vowels. Don't shout out your answer; just get it in your head. You can check our alphabet chart to see if Sarah's name has a, e, i, o, u, or y in it.

Call on students to identify the vowels that Sarah underlines with the red pen on your chart. Rewrite the name with the consonants in black and the vowel(s) in red. Repeat with several students.

Follow Up

Clap a student's name to listen for the parts or syllables. Tell students that each part of a name or a word has to have a vowel. Look at the student's name to see which vowels are in each syllable (example: Sar ah).

Using What You Know

In an independent word center, have students write high-frequency words and underline the vowels with a red pencil or pen.

* This vowel song is adapted from a song by Deb Teteris, First grade, Steinbeck Elementary, Fresno, California

Vowel Search

> **GRADE:** 1–2   **TIME:** 15–20 minutes
>
> **FOCUS:** To find vowels in words in the context of a familiar song or poem

Materials

* "Take Me Out to My Little League Game," page 92 (one per student) or any poem you currently are using in your pocket chart

* Eight sentence strips (or one for each line of the poem)

* Pocket chart

* Chart paper or whiteboard and two pens (one red)

* Pencils and paper and red crayons

Sequence

Teach

Choose a poem that your students have read many times.

> We know the poem "Take Me Out to My Little League Game" really well. Now let's use it to practice finding the vowels in the words. Remember our vowel song? We are looking for <u>a</u>, <u>e</u>, <u>i</u>, <u>o</u>, <u>u</u>, and sometimes <u>y</u> when it has a vowel sound.

Give examples of students' names, like *Bobby* or *Lynne*, or words like *my* or *baby*.

> Let's do the first line of the poem together, and then I will put you in groups to do the rest of the lines. Look at the top where it says <u>Take me out to my little league game</u>. I'll write the first word, <u>Take</u>, and you think quietly to yourself which letters are vowels.

Have students take turns coming up and marking under the vowels in red as you write each word. When they have the idea, move to group work.

Practice

Divide students into groups based on the number of lines left in the poem (seven in this example). Give each group one sentence strip with a line of the poem. Ask students to copy their line from the sentence strip and mark the vowels in red on scratch paper or in their Word Book. Students can help each other, and, if time allows, they can trade sentence strips with another group that is already done.

Follow Up

For further practice, students can individually mark a personal copy of the poem that you pass out.

Using What You Know

Use poetry or nursery rhymes in an independent poetry center. Invite students to copy words from the poem and underline the vowels in red.

Take Me Out to My Little League Game

Take me out to my little league game,

Take me out with my friends.

Buy me some nachos and soda pop,

I don't care if it ever ends.

With a cheer, cheer, cheer for my team,

If they don't win it's a shame.

For it's 1, 2, 3 strikes you're out,

At the old ball game.

What Is a Chunk?

GRADE: 1–2	**TIME:** 10–15 minutes

FOCUS: To establish that groups of letters go together to make sounds and that the brain looks for these patterns when reading unknown words

Materials

* Chart paper or whiteboard
* Two marking pens, (one red)
* *Scholastic Rhyming Dictionary* by Sue Young (recommended)

Sequence

Teach

Begin the lesson like this:

> *Boys and girls, I want you to pretend that I have chocolate in each of my hands.*

Extend your hands out, palms up to simulate holding candy in them.

> *If I was going to give you chocolate, which would you want? Little pieces (extend one hand) or a big chunk? (extend the other hand). That's right, most of you would want the biggest chunk possible—right? Well, that's what your brain wants when it comes to a word it doesn't know! Not little pieces, but big chunks of letters. So when we talk about chunking words we mean that your brain wants groups of letters that go together to make a sound. We have been learning about vowels* (refer to your alphabet chart with the vowels highlighted) *and most chunks start with a vowel.**

---

* In the purest definition, a rime, or chunk, is a vowel pattern in a syllable, but we also want readers to chunk groups of letters, such as digraphs (*sh, ch, th, wh*), and vowel patterns like diphthongs (*ou, oi, oy, ow*).

Practice

Begin the guided practice like this:

Let's practice using some chunks and see how many words have those chunks.

Write a chunk pattern on the chart paper or board in red. As students orally brainstorm words with that chunk, write them under the pattern with the consonants (onset) in black and the chunk (rime pattern that starts with the vowel and goes to the end of the word or syllable) in red. For example, you can write *rip* on the board, with *ip* in red. Then say, *If I know <u>rip</u>, I can read <u>sip</u>.* Write *sip* underneath *rip*, with the *ip* in red to highlight the chunk. Encourage students to brainstorm more words with the chunk, and write them underneath the first two examples. Repeat for each of the following chunks:

   it   *ug*   *at*   *est*   *op*

After you write a few for each one, consult the *Scholastic Rhyming Dictionary* for many more words with the patterns. Share these orally with the students.

So do you see that we can read and write lots of words if we know the chunk? Your brain helps you to read faster if you look and listen for the chunk—the letters that go together to make a sound.

Follow Up

If you have time, ask the students to write some simple words with the chunk patterns used above. Each time, they should underline the chunk with a red crayon so that they start to see it and hear it as a unit.

Using What You Know

Continue to point out common chunks that appear in shared reading and writing.

Break the Chunk

> **GRADE:** 1–2   **TIME:** 10–20 minutes (this can be modeled for the whole group but some students will need to practice in a smaller follow-up group)
>
> **FOCUS:** To take a word apart from left to right by consonants (onset) and the vowel pattern or chunk (rime)

Materials

* Magnetic letters: *a, c, t, s, p, l, f*
* Magnetic surface (see page 159)
* Chart paper or whiteboard and two colored pens (one red)
* Alphabet chart with the vowels highlighted

Sequence

Teach

Begin the lesson like this:

> *Boys and girls, sometimes when we are reading, we come to a word we don't know. A great way to figure out a tricky word is to break off the chunk at the end. It is easy to find the chunk in a word because it starts with a vowel.*

Refer to the alphabet chart and review the vowel song if necessary.

> *Watch me make the word <u>cat</u> and check it with my finger and eyes.*

Model how to make the word from left to right and go back and run your finger under it as you make the sounds /c/ /a/ /t/.

> *Check what I would do if this was a tricky word. I would take off the first letters up to the vowel <u>a</u> (pull off c and say /k/) and then read the chunk together (/at/). Now you take it apart.*

Have a student do this for the group, or, if you have a small group, have each student move the letters apart from left to right: *c-at*.

95

Then continue:

> *Watch now as I make a brand new word. I want you to tell me and show me how you would break it apart if you came upon it as a tricky word in reading.*

Make *scat* and solicit help breaking off the *sc-* (the letters up to the vowel) and the *at* (the chunk at the end of the word).

Practice

In small groups (perhaps after guided reading), have students break words apart. You make a word for them to copy but don't say the word aloud. Ask students to break off the consonant(s) up to the vowel first, then read the chunk as a unit. Words should be then read smoothly from left to right using both a finger and the eyes to check. Suggested words: *p-at, s-at, spl-at, f-at, fl-at*.

Follow Up

Pick some rhyming words out of a shared poem or Big Book, and ask students to break the words apart at the vowel pattern or chunk.

Using What You Know

In an independent word center, have students make the following words with magnetic letters and break them apart at the vowel chunk: *that, than, thank, they, then, them* (letters needed: *a, e, t, t, h, n, k, y, m*). Make sure students work left to right, as they do when reading.

light

hill

chin

ship

sit

sock

jump

skunk

Use the pictur
you read and
common spelli

from *Word Learning, Word Making, Word Sorting: 50 Lessons for Success* by Judy Lynch, Scholastic Professional Books, 2002
Illustrations by Yvette Banek

nine

ring

drink

smoke

stop

core

Chunk Chart

es and the vowel patterns shown in red to help

vrite new words. These are some of the most

ng patterns for reading and writing.

Learning the Chunk Chart

> **GRADE:** 1–2   **TIME:** 15–25 minutes
> review with short follow-up lessons
>
> **FOCUS:** To learn to use a chart with a key word and picture for
> the most common rime/chunk patterns found in words

Materials

* Chunk chart, page 99

* Words to "Take Me Out to My Little League Game," page 92, or any classroom
  Big Book or poem

* Chart paper or whiteboard and two colored pens (one red)

Sequence

Teach

Begin the lesson like this:

> *Look at our new chart that lists the most popular chunks found in words. Each
> chunk has a key word and picture to help us remember it when we come to
> tricky words in reading and writing. Let's learn the key pictures and words.*

Have an informal discussion about the pictures and words. Make sure they know what the
words mean and refer to the chunk and the word. For example:

> *Look at this backpack on our chart. How many of you bring a backpack to
> school? The key word is <u>backpack</u>. <u>ack</u>/<u>backpack</u>. What is the key word? (They
> should answer backpack.) What is the chunk? (ack.) That's right. Remember, we
> have been learning to break words apart at the vowel, which is the beginning
> of the chunk. What are some other <u>ack</u> words that <u>backpack</u> can help us read
> and spell?*

Orally brainstorm some *ack* words. Continue to learn the key words and the chunks in
them. This can be done for a few minutes every day so that it becomes a useful tool.

Practice

Begin the guided practice like this:

> *You know our chunk chart isn't just a pretty decoration for the wall. The key words remind us of chunks we can use to take words apart while reading and to build words when we are writing. Let's use our baseball poem and see how the chunks can help us read. If I didn't know _____ I could use _____ on the chart to help me figure out the word:*
>
>   *take/cake   win/chin   shame/game   at/bat*
>
> *Now help me write some words using the chart. Listen for the chunk: <u>stick</u>— what key word will help me write this? Yes, <u>chick</u> has the same <u>ick</u> chunk.*

Write *st* in a dark pen and the chunk, *ick*, in red. Continue with other examples:

    st**ar**/c**ar**   st**ore**/c**ore**   sk**ate**/pl**ate**

    tr**unk**/sk**unk**   fr**ight**/l**ight**   sp**elling**/sh**ell**/r**ing**

Follow Up

Over many days and weeks, refer to the chart during shared or guided reading and in writing. Look for students to start to internalize the chart and use it on their own to deconstruct (read) and construct (write) words. Encourage independence by prompting and praising them.

Using What You Know

In an independent Big Book center, have students find and record words that have the same chunk as the key words on the chart. Have them write the new word and the key word from the chart and underline the chunk in both words with a red crayon.

Example: str**ing**   r**ing**

Chunk Chart

back**p**ack	**p**ail	**r**ain	**c**ake	**g**ame	**p**an
car	t**r**ash	**b**at	**pl**ate	**s**aw	**pl**ay
meat	**sh**ell	**v**est	ice	**ch**ick	**sl**ide
light	**h**ill	**ch**in	**n**ine	**r**ing	d**r**ink
ship	**s**it	**s**ock	**sm**oke	**st**op	**c**ore
jump	**sk**unk				

Chunk Chart
Use the picture and the boldface vowel patterns to help you read and write new words. These are some of the most common spelling patterns for reading and writing.

Word Making With Chunks

GRADE: K–2	**TIME:** 15–25 minutes; this can be modeled for the whole group but is best done in a small group
	FOCUS: To use the chunk chart with its common rimes/vowel patterns to make words

Materials

* Paper or magnetic letters for each student: i, c, f, l, l, s, p, n, h (page 101)
* Chunk chart (page 99)
* Scratch paper and pencils, red crayons

Sequence

Teach

Begin the lesson like this:

> We're going to do word making today using two of the chunks from our chart: _ill/hill_ and _in/chin_. What chunks do we need to listen for? That's right, _ill_ and _in_.

Pass out letters and make sure everyone can see the chart.

Practice

Begin the guided practice like this:

> Take three letters and make _ill_. _I got ill and went to the school nurse._ _ill_. Run your finger under the word and check it slowly with your eyes. What is our key word for _ill_? Yes, _hill_.

> Add one letter and make _fill_. _Fill my glass with milk, please._ _fill_. What is the chunk? Yes, _ill_.

Now change the ending to make the three-letter word _fin_. _A fin helps a fish swim_. _fin_.

Let's change the first letter to make _pin_. _Don't stick me with a pin_. _pin_. What's the chunk? Yes, _in_. What is our key word on the chart for in? Yes, _chin_.

Let's change the ending and make the four-letter word _pill_. _The doctor gave me a pill_. _pill_. What's the chunk? Right. It's _ill_.

Change another letter now to make _sill_. _The edge of the window is the sill_. _sill_.

By adding a letter we can make the five-letter word _spill_. _Don't spill the milk_. _spill_. Is the chunk the same? Yes, it's still _ill_.

Now, use only four letters to make _spin_. _Spin the game wheel_. _spin_. What's the chunk? Right, it's _in_.

Let's change a couple letters (we still use four) to make _chin_. _I bumped my chin_. _chin_. Did the chunk change? No, it's still _in_.

Follow Up

Have students write a few words with these two chunk patterns and underline the chunk with a red crayon. Dictate and use in a sentence: _still, grin, dill, twin, drill_.

Using What You Know

In an independent poetry center, have students find words with the _in_ and _ill_ chunks in them. For example: the nursery rhymes "Little Boy Blue" and "Ding Dong Bell."

For more word making lessons using both the most common short and long vowel patterns, see my first book, _Easy Lessons for Teaching Word Families_, Scholastic Inc., 1998.

i	c	f	l	l
s	p	n	h	

Word Sorting With Chunks

GRADE: K–2 **TIME:** 10–20 minutes

FOCUS: To read and sort words by looking at the beginning consonant(s) (onset) and chunking the vowel pattern at the end of the word or syllable (rime).

Materials

* Chunk chart (page 99)

* Copies of word sheet on page 104

* Copies of four-column sorting mat on page 157; label columns *car, sit, pot,* and *No Match*

* Scissors and glue or paste

Sequence

Teach

Review the chunk chart with the class (do this often to make it a usable tool).

> *Let's do some fast practice with our Chunk Chart. I will point to a picture and you will say the chunk and the key word. For example if I point here* (ship) *you will say ip, ship.*

Point to a variety of pictures, stressing short vowel patterns for now. Students should respond with the chunk and the key word.

> *Today for word sorting, we will sort for the chunks ar like in car, it as in sit, and ot, like in pot.*

Show them the sorting mat with these key words at the top.

> *You will have to look carefully because there will be some words with no match; I am trying to trick you! We know that good readers LOOK ACROSS A WORD, but today I want you to also CHUNK THE WORD. You know that after*

the consonant(s) at the beginning of a word, a vowel starts the chunk. Look for the vowel and then to the end of the word to get the whole chunk.

Demonstrate with key words on the chunk chart how to sound out up to the vowel and then chunk the word.

Practice

Pass out copies of the word sheet (page 104) and sorting mat. Judge the level of support your students need. If they need extra help seeing the pattern at the end of the word, monitor them as they highlight each chunk with yellow highlighter pens. Otherwise proceed as below:

Let's read our words today before you begin to sort. Remember to sound out the consonant(s) at the beginning and then chunk the end starting with the vowel.

Have them read the words together and run their fingers under the letters from left to right while *looking* carefully at each letter.

Now cut your words out, sort by the chunks, and glue them down on your sorting mat.

Follow Up

Dictate these words for students to write: *mar, hot, flit.* (Or have them try others with these patterns.) Can they connect these patterns to writing with them?

Using What You Know

In an independent word center, place extra copies of the sorting mat you created for *ar, it,* and *ot.* Have students write more words with the pattern and underline the chunk in red

Future Sorting by:	ash	an	at	ick	ill	in	ug	ump	unk
SHORT VOWEL CHUNKS	cash	tan	hat	stick	still	tin	jug	jump	junk
Use the blank sorting boxes on	slash	Nan	cat	brick	bill	bin	tug	trump	trunk
page 154 to create new word	smash	Stan	scat	pick	pill	pin	slug	slump	sunk
sorts using short vowel chunks.									
Include three words that do not	**op**	**ack**	**ock**	**est**	**ell**	**ill**			
go into any category and will be	stop	stack	stock	best	bell	bill			
placed under "No Match."	top	tack	tock	nest	fell	fill			
	flop	rack	rock	crest	spell	spill			

lit	cat	bar	not
star	lot	spit	hat
shot	jar	spot	fit
hit	jam	stop	tar
mop	scar	tot	split

Word Learning Word Making Word Sorting: 50 Lessons for Success *Scholastic Professional Books*

Writing and Reading With Chunks

> **GRADE:** K–2   **TIME:** 10–25 minutes (repeat often so students use the chart flexibly as a spelling and writing tool)
>
> **FOCUS:** To listen to patterns and write them using the chunk chart as a tool

Materials

* Chunk chart (page 99)
* Whiteboards or scratch paper
* Pens or pencils
* Highlighter pens or red crayons

Sequence

Teach

Begin the lesson like this:

> Let's do a quick review of our chunk chart today. I will say a word, and you listen for the chunk. Then we will find the key word that will help us to spell and write new words. Don't shout out your answer; keep it in your head. When you think you know the key word that matches the word I say, smile at me so I can see who knows the answer.
>
> Listen to this: <u>Nat is a boy's name. Nat.</u> (**bat**, **at**) What chunk do you hear? That's right, <u>at</u>. Let's find <u>at</u> on the chunk chart and read the key word—<u>bat</u>.

Do several examples to demonstrate this new way to use the chart. Try these words: *fin, bunk, best, tack, top.*

Practice

Begin the guided practice like this:

Listen carefully. I will say a word, use it in a sentence, and say it again. It will have the same chunk as one of the key words from our chunk chart. You need to find the key word and see how the chunk is spelled; remember the chunk usually starts with the first vowel in a word. The word I want you to write will have different letters at the beginning. Write the new sounds; then write the chunk. Check the word carefully with your finger and your eyes as you sound it out. Does it look right? Then highlight the chunk (or underline it with red crayon).

bump.	I have a bump on my head.	bump.
man.	The man visited our class.	man.
sill.	The sill is the bottom edge of the window.	sill.
bell.	The bell will ring for recess.	bell.
rug.	Wipe your muddy feet on the rug.	rug

Continue as time permits. Do this often as both a class and in smaller groups after reading a story

Follow Up

Have students work in pairs practicing words from the chart. They can take turns giving a key word while their partner tries to write it without using the chart.

Using What You Know

In an independent word center, have students write more words with the same chunks or patterns as in the examples above. Make sure they highlight each chunk or underline it in red crayon.

Find the Chunk

> **GRADE:** K–2   **TIME:** 10–20 minutes
>
> **FOCUS:** To find chunks in regular classroom reading
> material through regular use of the chunk chart

Materials

✳ Chunk Chart (page 99)

✳ *Clap Your Hands* (Big Book) by Lorinda Bryan Cauley, Scholastic Inc., 1992 or any Big
Book or poem you are currently using with your class

✳ Highlighter tape or wikki stix

✳ Chart paper or whiteboard and pens

Sequence

Teach

Begin the lesson like this:

> *Okay, class, let's do a quick review of how to use our chunk chart for read-
> ing words we don't know. I'll show you a word that you might find in a book
> or poem, and I want you to use our chart to read the new word.*

> *When I write the word, don't blurt out the answer. I want everyone to have
> time to think. I'll call on someone sitting quietly; you can show me you have
> the answer in your head by nodding your head yes.*

Write the word *crop*. Check that students are using the chart and wait for them to nod
their head yes before calling for the answer: *stop/op*.

> *Good. Now let's read the beginning of the new word and add the chunk <u>op</u>
> like in <u>stop</u>. cr-op.*

Practice with several other words: *smell, chat, smug.*

It's time to use this in our Big Book <u>Clap Your Hands</u>. Sometimes we come to a word we don't know, and we can use our chunk chart. Even if you do know the words in the book today, that's okay because we are learning a strategy to use with words we don't know. You'll be able to use it with lots of other words.

Practice

Read through several pages of the book. When a word has the same chunk as one of the key words on the chunk chart, stop, and have a student mark it with highlighter tape or frame it with their fingers or wikki stix. Use the chunk to read the new word in the book. Please note that there will be many words with less common chunks that appear in books. Later, students can apply the strategy of CHUNKING THE WORD to any new word without a chart. The chart helps us to start with the most common patterns. Here's a line of text from *Clap Your Hands* with the chunks in bold to reference from the chart: *Sh**ake** your arms, then t**ake** a s**eat**.*

> sh**ake**/c**ake**/**ake**
>
> **ar**ms/c**ar**/**ar**
>
> t**ake**/c**ake**/**ake**
>
> s**eat**/m**eat**/**eat**

Follow Up

Challenge students to brainstorm more words from your sample words: *crop, smell, chat,* and *smug.* They should write them down and underline the chunk in red crayon.

Using What You Know

Put your Big Book or poem in an independent word center. Invite students to look for more words in the text that have the same chunks as those on the chart. They should record the new word, the key word, and underline the chunk in both in red crayon in their Word Books.

What Do I Know?: Using the Chart

GRADE: 1–2 **TIME:** 15–20 minutes; repeat the strategy *often* with other words

FOCUS: To learn words by analogy, using something students know to figure out something new

Materials

❋ Chunk chart (page 99)

❋ Chart paper or whiteboard and pens (one red)

Sequence

Teach

Begin the lesson like this:

Let's review our chunk chart for a few minutes. I'll write a word, and you tell me which key word will help you to read it.

Write *stack, chest, fight, slop,* and *stump* one at a time. Have students come up and identify the key word, say the chunk that it reminds them of, and sound out the new word using the chunk they know.

That was easy because we have been doing short words. But when you are reading, you will find longer words with more parts, or syllables. I can't possibly teach you all the words there are, but I can teach you how to figure out tricky words. I want you to look at a word you think is hard and ask your WHAT DO I KNOW? When you find chunks you already know, then the word is easier than you think it will be.

I have some longer words for you to practice reading today. Each one will have two chunks from our chart. Let's try the first one together. (Write testing.) Remember that there are two chunks. Let's look at the beginning

of the word and find the first chunk. Ask yourself, WHAT DO I KNOW? What is the first vowel? (They should answer e.) After the e what do you see that could be a chunk?

If needed, go to the chunk chart and look at the key words where the vowel is e (*meat/eat, shell/ell, vest/est*).

I can use est like in vest so what is the first part of the word—t-est? Underline the est in red.

Now ask yourself again when you look at the ending, WHAT DO I KNOW? (ring/ing). Just put them together: test-ing, testing.

Practice

Here are more words to practice this strategy. Always explain what the words mean to build vocabulary and have students repeat them aloud after you've written them on the board. Coach and give support over many short practice sessions so that students learn to use the chunk chart on more complex words.

instill	haystack	blacktop	cockpit	dingbat
pancake	inflame	nickname	Batman	lawman
backlash	ice skate	playmate	tailgate	stingray
backseat	trick or treat	invest	chopstick	nitpick
inside	riptide	catfight	daylight	flashlight
starlight	stoplight	trash can	tailspin	snakeskin
incline	kinship	cockpit	tick tock	bellhop
hilltop	raindrop	cannot	jackpot	chipmunk

Follow Up

After each practice session, invite students to write the words they've read aloud in the above lesson. To do this, erase the words you wrote and say them aloud. Have students listen for the first chunk in the first syllable and record its spelling. Then give them the chunk in the second syllable, have them check the chart, and record it in their Word Books. Careful—writing and spelling can be harder than reading these words!

Using What You Know

In all guided and shared reading, look for opportunities to use your chart on longer words. Even if only one chunk in a two-syllable word is on the chart, show them how to use that and have them chunk the rest as best they can. This takes lots of modeling and practice.

What Do I Know?

> **GRADE:** 1–2   **TIME:** 15–20 minutes; repeat with many short lessons while reading and writing
>
> **FOCUS:** To use part of an unknown word to solve the whole word, with or without the chunk chart

Materials

* Chunk chart (page 99)
* Chart paper or whiteboard and pens (one red)

Sequence

Teach

Begin the lesson like this

> *We have been using our chunk chart to figure out tricky words. Remember, we ask ourselves, WHAT DO I KNOW? when we aren't sure of a word. Sometimes part of the word is like a key word on our chart. But our chunk chart has only a few of the chunks in the hundreds of words we read. Today I want to show you how we can still look for what we know even if it's not on the chart. Here's a key word from our chart.*

Write *bug.*

> *What is the chunk?*

Underline *ug* in red.

> *We have learned that we can make more words from this chunk.*

Write a few more words under *bug,* like *hug* and *mug.*

> *What I want you to notice today is that there are chunks like ug that we can figure out without our chart. For example, this word has a chunk that is a little like ug.*

111

Write *yum* on the board.

> *Can you find the chunk in this new word?*

Help them look for the first vowel and read to the end of the word; then underline *um* in red.

> *What is our new chunk? (They should say um.) So, what is our new word? (yum.) Can you read this word?*

Write *gum* under *yum*.

> *Here's another chunk that is a little like our key word, bug.*

Write *fun*.

> *If you know the chunk ug in bug, you can figure out this new chunk.*

Underline *un* when they find the chunk.

> *And you can read lots of words like fun.*

Write *run* and *sun* for them to compare.

> *So we see that we can't always find the key word on the chart. But we can still find parts we know and CHUNK THE WORD. Let's practice some more words we can chunk without our chunk chart.*

Practice

Write more words for students to chunk. Refer to similar words (shown in parentheses) on the chunk chart if needed.

b**ike**(sl**ide**)   h**im**(ch**in**)   s**and**(p**an**)   b**ark**(c**ar**)

l**ed**(sh**ell**)   fr**og**(st**op**)   f**ork**(c**ore**)   d**uck**(b**ug**)

s**ung**(sk**unk**)

Follow Up

Ask students to write a few one-syllable words from the samples above (erase or cover your writing) and to mark the chunk in red. Remember that writing can be more challenging than reading new words; remind students to listen carefully.

Using What You Know

Encourage students to look for short words with new chunks in their guided or shared reading stories. In an independent word center, invite them to record the words in their Word Books and underline the chunk(s) in red crayon.

Word Sorting by "What I Know"

GRADE: 1–2   **TIME:** 15–20 minutes

FOCUS: To use known parts of words to chunk and decode unknown words

Materials

* Chart paper or whiteboard and pens (one red)
* Copies of four-column sorting mat on page 157; label columns *ing*, *th*, *all*, and *No Match*
* Word sheet on page 115
* Scissors and glue or paste

Sequence

Teach

Begin the lesson like this:

Today we are going to do a harder word sorting. We'll have to look very carefully to find what we know and use all three of our main strategies for figuring out a tricky word. We will LOOK ACROSS THE WORD quickly and ask, WHAT DO I KNOW? Then we'll use what we know to CHUNK THE WORD.

Write the word *Thanksgiving*.

Sometimes what we know is at the beginning of a word, like /th/ (underline Th in red). Sometimes the part we know is at the end of a tricky word, like /ing/ (underline ing in red). And sometimes the part we know is buried in the middle, like /ank/ (underline ank in red).

113

Let's LOOK ACROSS THE WORD. We have already underlined WHAT I KNOW; now we can CHUNK THE WORD.

Model how to chunk and blend the word *Thanksgiving*. If students already know this sample word, remind them we are using it to review our strategies to use on words they won't know.

Practice

Begin the guided practice like this:

The words on this page (pass out page 115) have some parts you already know hidden among other letters. Usually we read our sorting words first, but today we will wait to read them until we are done gluing them down. We are looking for these parts we know in words: <u>ing</u>, <u>th</u>, <u>all</u>.

Pass out the 4-column sorting mat.

Remember that if you don't see any of these chunks in a word, put it in the last column for <u>No Match</u>. *Are your eyes ready to look closely for what you know? Okay, get started.*

Follow Up

When students are done sorting, lead them in blending the chunks to read each word smoothly. Many words will need to be discussed for their meanings

Using What You Know

Encourage students to use all three strategies in taking apart unknown words in guided and shared reading. This move into solving longer words takes much modeling by the teacher and coaching while students are reading.

tallest	shiner	mother	springs
running	thick	small	valentine
month	pinch	giving	ballboy
squall	stinger	gather	tell
fifth	caller	dingdong	caller

Word Sliders With Simple Chunks

GRADE: 1–2   **TIME:** 15–20 minutes to make materials;
10–15 minutes to teach the task
(this can be a two-day lesson).

FOCUS: To match beginning consonants (onsets) with short
vowel chunks (rimes) to generate word families and
sort real and made-up words

Materials

* Scissors, tape, a small envelope for each student and staplers
* Consonant list, page 120
* Simple chunk cards, pages 118–119
* Scratch paper or personal Word Books and pencils
* *The Scholastic Rhyming Dictionary* (Scholastic 1994)
  by Sue Young (recommended)

Run copies of the Consonant List for each student on card
stock. Cut apart the three columns and tape into one long
strip, making a vertical slider. (See photo at right.)

Make copies of both pages of simple chunk cards for each
student on cardstock. Have students cut carefully to make
individual cards. Make a pile of chunks with the vowel *a*,
making sure they know there are three sounds of *a* here:
short *a* (*ack, an, ash, at*), long *a* (*ay*); short *o* (*ar, aw*).
Continue with a pile for *e, i, o,* and *u* until you have five piles.

As students finish, have them read independently while you and trusted helpers staple the
chunk cards together. Put a staple in the top right corner of each stack so that the cards

can be folded back to show other chunks for word making. Students can keep their chunk cards in a small envelope with their name on it.

Sequence

Teach

Begin the lesson like this:

> *I want to show you how to use our sliders to make lots of words. I hold the slider with the consonants in my left hand. I take my chunk cards and turn to the one I want to use. Today I will use at. I will start at the top of the consonants with the b and see if that makes a word with at. /b/ + /at/ = /bat/. Now I have to see if /bat/ is a real word. What is a bat?*

Students should get this from the chunk chart. Continue with /cat/ /dat/ /fat/ /gat/, and so on. Students will need lots of help figuring out the "Dr. Seuss words"—words that rhyme but are made up, as are often found in these favorite children's books. At first students will think that if they can say it and it rhymes, it must be a word. Question them: "What is a *dat?*" "What is a *gat?*"

Practice

Ask students to work in small groups to practice a pattern you give them, such as *ash*. They should slide the chunk down the side of the consonants and then discuss whether the combination makes a word. If students agree it is a real word (not a Dr. Seuss word), they can record it on their scratch paper or in their word books. Doing this together helps them to sort out real (*dash*) and made-up (*fash*) words. They will get some of these mixed up, but you should check in on them to correct if necessary. Even made-up words give them sound-blending practice. You can also have groups compare the words they've written down.

Follow Up

Show students how these simple patterns can make larger compound and multi-syllabic words. Come up with your own examples or look up a pattern in *The Scholastic Rhyming Dictionary*. Do this often so they don't think *at* is just for *cat* but can also be found in *thermostat*.

Using What You Know

Look for words that come up in guided and shared reading lessons that have these simple chunk patterns. Refer to the chunk cards as another link to these common word families.

ar	an	ack
aw	at	ash
est	ell	ay
	ill	ick

Word Learning Word Making Word Sorting: 50 Lessons for Success *Scholastic Professional Books*

ink	ock	ug	
ing	it	at	unk
in	ip	op	ump

Word Learning Word Making Word Sorting: 50 Lessons for Success *Scholastic Professional Books*

b	k	s
c	l	t
d	m	v
f	n	w
g	p	x
h	qu	y
j	r	z

Word Learning Word Making Word Sorting: 50 Lessons for Success *Scholastic Professional Books*

Chapter 4

Embedded Letters and Letter Clusters

*I*n previous chapters, students moved from attending to whole-word units to looking at sub-word parts (initial and final letters, suffixes, and simple chunks). In this chapter, the emphasis will be on teaching them to think about and look for embedded letters and letter clusters. As Judith Neal reminds us, don't assume that students' eyes can do this "picking apart" automatically. The skill needs to be taught explicitly and discussed during reading and writing lessons.

Why are embedded letter clusters the most difficult for students to process? Marie Clay (1991) explains that "a child finds the beginnings and ends of words easier to 'see' than features embedded within sentences or words. The spaces help him to locate and perceive the letter at the edges of the spaces." So the spaces between words make it easier for a child's eyes to notice the letters close to those spaces—sub-word parts. The goal of this chapter is to teach students to look into words.

Embedded information also can be more complex because words can contain consonant and vowel clusters, complex vowel patterns, and multiple syllables. The lessons in this chapter review key strategies, such as LOOKING ACROSS A WORD, and asking, WHAT DO I KNOW? We will now build flexibility with letter sounds, especially vowels, by teaching students to ask, WHAT OTHER SOUND CAN I TRY? when confronted with a vowel that has multiple sounds (*cat, Kate, all, away,* for example). Our goal for students is to become fluent enough so that they can use letter clusters to take words apart in reading and construct words in writing.

Like the other lessons in this book, use these as a model to teach strategies that students can employ with increasingly more complex words in stories. The best place for these lessons is in the context of your regular reading and writing instruction. For students to internalize these word-learning strategies fully, they'll need to practice them over many guided reading and writing lessons.

In the 1999 movie *At First Sight,* Val Kilmer played a blind man whose sight is restored by an operation. He became frustrated, however, because he continued to bump into things he could see. His doctor reminded him that even though he could now see, *he had to learn to look.* That is the underpinning of the word learning, word making, and word sorting lessons in this chapter. Just because children see a word while reading, it doesn't mean that they are looking carefully into the word. Let's teach them to do just that!

What's Different? Looking Into Words

> **GRADE:** 1–2   **TIME:** 15–20 minutes
>
> **FOCUS:** To look into words for the details that make them different from other words

Materials

* Chart paper or overhead projector, pens (one red)
* Scratch paper or personal word books for each student to record dictated words
* Pencils and red crayons for each student
* Ten three-by-five-inch index cards with the words: *cup, cut, map, mop, stop, step, pit, pet, pan,* and *pat*

Sequence

Teach

Begin the lesson like this:

> *When we are reading stories, some of the hardest words are very small. What makes them tricky is that they look very much like another word you know. If you don't LOOK INTO THE WORD, you might say the wrong word. You need to sharpen your eyes and notice what is different in the inside of the word. We'll start by writing some words that are almost the same. Later, I will have you read these words very fast, so be ready to look closely at them.*

Model the following process first on your chart paper or overhead by saying and then writing *then*, *them*, and *than*. Underline what is different. Next, dictate a pair of words for the students to write on their scratch paper or in their Word Books. Then ask, "What is different?" about each pair. Have students underline the unique features in red.

Practice

Repeat the process you've modeled above with these word pairs: *cup/cut, map/mop, stop/step, pit/pet,* and *pan/pat.*

When students have finished writing the words and underlining the parts that are different in red, collect their papers and cover up the work you have done on your chart paper.

Follow Up

For a quick follow-up, try this:

> *Now that we have written these words, it is time to read them quickly, like you have to do when reading them in a book. You need to LOOK INTO THE WORD and quickly notice all the letters. Ready? Let's see how fast you can read these word cards. I'll have someone different read each card aloud while the rest of you keep the word in your heads.*

Shuffle the cards dramatically and quickly flash them at individuals. The other students must keep the word in their heads. Do this repeatedly and quickly, involving all students.

Using What You Know

In an independent center, have students make the ten words you've reviewed with magnetic letters and record them once more in their Word Books.

Look Into the Word: Vowel Sorting

> **GRADE:** 1–2 **TIME:** 20–25 minutes
>
> **FOCUS:** To teach students to look into a word to find embedded letters or clusters

Materials

* Alphabet chart, page 53
* Copies of word sheet on page 127
* Copies of five-column sorting mat on page 158; label columns *a, e, i, o,* and *u*
* Chart or whiteboard and pens (one red)
* Scissors and glue or paste

Sequence

Teach

Begin the lesson like this:

> *Today you had better have very sharp eyes to do word sorting. I have chosen words that look the same at the beginning and at the end. That means you have to LOOK INTO THE WORD to find what part is different. * We will be sorting words by the five vowels, a̲, e̲, i, o, and u̲. Who can find them on our alphabet chart?*

As various students point out the vowels, take time to discuss what each vowel looks like, its unique visual features.

> *Here are some words to practice with.*

Write *him, ham, hum,* and *hem.*

---

* Thanks to Dr. Judith Neal for the reminder of how important it is for students to LOOK INTO A WORD for information at this point in the word-learning process.

These words look so much alike we have to LOOK INTO THE WORD to tell them apart. Read them with me, and we'll look for what's different.

As the group reads the words, underline the vowels in red and discuss word meanings to build vocabulary. Then, show the sorting mat for today's lesson and ask where each word (*him*, *ham*, *hum*, and *hem*) should go, under which vowel it should appear.

Practice

Begin the guided practice like this:

Let's look at the words we will sort today and read them to ourselves.

Pass out the word sheets and monitor as students read the words independently.

Cut your words apart and stack them in piles that start with the same letter. Put all the b words together, all the n words together, and all the s words together. Now, look into each word. See which vowel is in the middle and read it again softly to yourself. Glue each word under a, e, i, o, or u.

Follow Up

Make up word cards for these words (use the template below). See if students can read them quickly: *then, than, thin; mask, musk; strap, strip, strep.*

Using What You Know

In an independent literacy center, have students practice writing the words that they have sorted by vowels.

then	thin	musk	strip
than	mask	strap	strep

bag	bog	big	bug
beg	ball	bill	bell
bit	but	bet	bull
nut	Nat	net	nit
spot	spit	spat	not

Vowels Have Different Sounds

GRADE: 1–2   **TIME:** 15–20 minutes; repeat with many
short reviews

FOCUS: To build an awareness of short and long vowel sounds
to teach students to be flexible in trying these sounds

Materials

* Alphabet chart, page 53
* Chunk chart, page 99
* Whiteboard or chart paper and pens (one red)
* Scratch paper or personal word books, plus pencils and red crayons

Sequence

Teach

Begin the lesson like this:

> We have used our alphabet chart to learn the names and sounds of the letters.
> But I'm sure you have noticed that some letters have more than one sound,
> especially the vowels.

> The sounds of the vowels on our chart are called short vowel sounds. Say
> them with me: /a/, <u>apple</u>; /e/, <u>elephant</u>; /i/, <u>igloo</u>; /o/, <u>octopus</u>; /u/, <u>umbrella</u>. All
> of these vowels have other sounds. When we come to a word we don't know,
> we have to look at the vowels, and the chunks they are in, very carefully.

> The silent <u>e</u> at the end of a word makes a new chunk in that word and many
> times changes the vowel to a long vowel sound.

The "silent e" only makes the vowel long in about 60 percent of words. Be careful that this isn't taught as a rule; we want students to be flexible and to try other vowel sounds when the one they are trying doesn't sound right.

> *Look on our chunk chart: <u>cake</u>, <u>game</u>, <u>plate</u>, <u>ice</u>, <u>slide</u>, <u>nine</u>, <u>smoke</u>. The chunk for <u>cake</u> is <u>ake</u>, not <u>ak</u>. Wouldn't it sound funny to read a story about a birthday party that talked about kids eating <u>cak</u>? It doesn't make sense, does it? The silent <u>e</u> in <u>ake</u> changes the sound of the vowel <u>a</u>. It does the same for <u>ice</u>, <u>smoke</u>, and others.*

Check to be sure your students see and hear the changes in other words from the chart. Stress the letter/sound unit of the chunk changes, not just the vowel. We want them to continue to focus on the pattern.

Practice

Begin the guided practice like this:

> *Let's write and read some words with and without the silent <u>e</u>. We'll compare how they look and sound.*

Pass out paper and pencils. Students will also need a red crayon to underline the vowel pattern. Dictate the following words, and ask students to underline the chunks and compare how they look and sound: *pan/pane, cut/cute, bit/bite, pet/Pete, hop/hope.*

Follow Up

Be alert to silent e chunks in words that come up in shared and guided reading. Point out the vowel sound changes.

Using What You Know

In an independent word center, have students find silent e chunks in words they read in books. They should record the words and underline the chunks in red crayon or yellow highlighter pen.

Word Making With Long and Short Vowels

GRADE: 1–2	TIME: 15–20 minutes

FOCUS: To use silent e patterns to review that vowels have different sounds and to reinforce the strategy: WHAT OTHER SOUND CAN I TRY?

Materials

* Alphabet chart, page 53
* Letters for each student: *a, e, f, h, n, m, r, t* (page 132)
* Whiteboard or chart paper and pens (one red)
* Three-by-five-inch word cards: *fat, fate, Nate, Nat, rat, rate, mate, mat, hate, hat*

Sequence

Teach

Review vowels, referring to the vowel chart.

> *Do vowels have more than one sound in words? Yes, they do. And we know that if we read a word that doesn't sound like a word we know, we need to ask ourselves, WHAT OTHER SOUND CAN I TRY? Look at this word (write bit). Does it have a chunk you know?*

Refer to the chunk chart with the key word *sit*.

> *If you know it/sit, what is this word?*

They should say *bit*. Then add an e to the end to make *bite*.

> *Is it bit now? Let's think: WHAT OTHER SOUND CAN I TRY? Right, the chunk*

has changed to _ite_, and the vowel has a new sound. What is it? /i/—yes, when the letter has the sound of its name, like _i_, that's called the long vowel sound.

Underline the _it_ in _bit_ and the _ite_ in _bite_ with red to highlight the chunks.

Practice

Begin the guided practice this:

Now let's make words with long and short vowel sounds. Watch for silent letters.

First, let's take three letters and make _fat_. _The little puppy was fat._ _fat_. What is the chunk? (They should respond with at/bat from the chunk chart.)

Add one letter and make _fate_. _It was fate that they met._ _fate_. How many sounds do you hear? How many letters do you need? Is the new chunk like _ate/plate_ on the chunk chart?

Let's change one letter to make _Nate_. _Nate is a boy's name._ _Nate_. What is the chunk? Is it the same as the last one?

Use three letters to make _Nat_. _Nat can be a boy's name, too._ _Nat_. Did you need the _e_?

Let's change another letter to make rat. _The rat is white._ rat. Does the _a_ sound like the name of the letter?

Add a letter to make _rate_. _The car went at a fast rate._ _rate_. Do you hear the letter name _a_?

Does the chunk _ate_ have the long vowel sound?

Now let's change a letter to make _mate_. _I lost the mate to my shoe._ _mate_. What's the chunk?

We only need three letters to make _mat_. _Wipe your feet on the mat._ _mat_. That has the short _a_ sound.

We need to use four letters to make _hate_. _I hate spinach._ _hate_. How many sounds do you hear? What is the chunk?

If we use three letters, we can make _hat_. _I have a cowboy hat._ _hat_. Which letter did you take away?

Follow Up

Sort words by long and short vowel sounds. Then dictate more word pairs with the silent e for students to write. Tell the students how many letters to use, dictate the word, and then ask them how many sounds they hear. This practice cues them to silent letters. Sample words: *pan/pane, kite/kit, tine/tin, Sam/same.*

Using What You Know

Over time, collect silent e words from books and poetry on a chart. Sort them into long and other vowel categories. Examples: *mate, give.* See sample list below.

<u>long</u>	<u>other</u>
coke	have
like	are
cake	one
cube	come
late	were
bite	there

a	e	f	h
n	m	r	t

Word Sorting With Long and Short Vowels

GRADE: 1–2	**TIME:** 20–25 minutes

FOCUS: To learn to be flexible reading unknown and to ask, WHAT OTHER SOUND CAN I TRY? if the first vowel doesn't make a word

Materials

* Copies of three-column sorting mat page 156; label columns *long vowel*, *short vowel*, and *No Match*

* Copies of word sheet on page 136

* Scissors and glue or paste

* Alphabet chart, page 53

* Three-by-five-inch word cards for: *pan, pane, cut, cute, bit, bite, pet, Pete, hop, hope*

Sequence

Teach

Begin the lesson like this:

> *We are going to sort words with long and short vowel sounds. The short vowel sounds are in <u>cat</u>, <u>elephant</u>, <u>igloo</u>, <u>octopus</u>, and <u>umbrella</u>.*

Emphasize the vowel sounds as you say these key words.

> *Let's try some words and compare the short and long vowel sounds. <u>The little bunny will . . .</u>*

Show the card for *hop* and lead them in sounding it out.

Does that sound like a word that tells about a bunny? Would it fit to say <u>The little bunny will . . .</u>

Show the card for *hope* and lead them in sounding it out.

<u>Hope</u> doesn't make sense there, does it? How did the word <u>hop</u> change when the silent <u>e</u> was added to make <u>hope</u>? Let's try some others.

Compare *pan/pane, cut/cute, bit/bite,* and *pet/Pete* by making sentences. Make sure students know that in the long vowel chunk (*ane, ute, ite, ete*) the first vowel sounds like the name of the vowel itself.

The silent <u>e</u> doesn't always change the vowel sound from short to long (give them the example have*), but many times the first vowel sound in the chunk does change. When you are sounding out a new word, try the vowel sound you think is right, and if that doesn't make a word ask yourself, WHAT OTHER SOUND CAN I TRY?*

Practice

Begin the guided practice like this:

Before you sort your words, let's very carefully read them. If the first time we read a word it doesn't sound like a real word, let's ask, WHAT OTHER SOUND CAN I TRY?

Go through the words slowly, coaching the students to pay attention to the short and long vowel sounds. Pass out the word sheets and sorting mats and ask students to cut apart the words; then they can sort them on the mats, gluing words in the appropriate columns. If students are not yet ready to do this independently, continue to give them support. Otherwise, have the students work by themselves, and monitor their efforts. They should be able to read the words to you.

Follow Up

During guided and shared reading, look for opportunities to model for a group or individual how to try other vowel sounds when a word they read doesn't sound right or make sense. To be flexible they must learn to ask, WHAT OTHER SOUND CAN I TRY?

Using What You Know

In an independent word center, give each student another copy of the blank sorting mat for long and short vowel words (use the template on page 156 and label the columns:

long vowel, *short vowel*, and *No Match*). Have students record words they find in stories the class has read in guided or shared reading. Each word should be gone over carefully and then recorded in the correct column.

Future Sorting by: EMBEDDED/ LONG VOWEL WORD CHUNKS

Use the blank sorting boxes on page 154 to create new word sorts using long vowel chunks or patterns. Be sure to include three words that do not go into any category and will be placed under *No Match*.

ate	ain	ay	ide	ight	ine	oke	ake	ore
rate	rain	ray	slide	slight	shine	smoke	snake	snore
plate	pain	play	bride	bright	brine	choke	cake	chore
gate	train	tray	stride	fright	spine	broke	brake	bore

eat	ate	ice	ude	ue	ule
meat	mate	mice	dude	due	mule
seat	slate	slice	crude	true	yule
treat	rate	twice	prude	glue	rule

---

smoke	stock	boil	quake
cow	stroke	whine	smock
slice	thick	crook	quack
the	win	stride	thrice
flake	scat	flock	slick

What Others Sound Can I Try?

GRADE: 1–2   **TIME:** 15–20 minutes; repeat with many short follow-up lessons

FOCUS: To use the WHAT OTHER SOUND CAN I TRY? strategy

Materials

❋ Whiteboard or chart paper and pens

Sequence

Teach

Begin the lesson like this:

> Today I have some words for you to read that are just like words we read in books. We know that vowels have lots of sounds, which can be tricky. It helps to remember to try a new sound when we read a word and we know something is wrong.

> For our practice today, I am using two different sounds for <u>oo</u>. Here's our first word to figure out (write bookworm). I know that I'm supposed to ask WHAT DO I KNOW? Who can help me find a part we know to help us?

Encourage any responses to known parts. Most likely, someone will point out the word book.

> <u>Book</u> is a part we know, and it is also a key word to remind us that one sound of two <u>o</u>'s together is like in <u>book</u>. Let's use that to read the whole word: <u>bookworm</u>.

Write the word *book* on top of your chart.

> Here is another word with two <u>o</u>'s.

137

Write the word *zooming*.

> *Let's see if it sounds like <u>book</u>.*

Exaggerate reading it with the wrong sound.

> *Remember, if that doesn't make a word, we ask, WHAT OTHER SOUND CAN I TRY?*

Write *zoo* at the top of the chart.

> *Here is another key word to remind us of another sound for two <u>o</u>'s. If we know <u>zoo</u>, how do we chunk this word (point to <u>zooming</u>)?*

Work out the word with the group.

> *So now we know that letters can have more than one sound, especially vowels. If we are ready to try other sounds, words can't trick us. Let's try some more.*

Practice

Write these words one at a time for the group to work out:

scooter	moose	spoofed	troops
crooked	stood	woody	goodness
stoops	shooting	stools	swooning

Have students keep the answer in their heads to prevent a few from shouting it out and spoiling the strategy practice for all. (Remind them, even if they know the word, that what is most important is to learn how to use the strategy.) For each word, try the sound of **bo**o**k**, ask WHAT OTHER SOUND CAN I TRY? and try the sound of **zoo**. Ask them which makes a word. Use the unknown word in a sentence if needed to build meaning.

Follow Up

Practice this strategy for flexibility with *ow* words, using c**ow** and sn**ow** as the key words. Sample words: *drowning, mower, growing, crowns, prowler, shown.*

Using What You Know

Invite students to be word detectives and to find more words in guided and shared reading books with the double o pattern. Record them under the key words *book* and *zoo*.

What Others Sound Can I Try?
Sorting by Vowel Sounds

GRADE: 1–2   **TIME:** 20–25 minutes (this is the basic format for five lessons, each using a different vowel

FOCUS: To learn to be flexible when reading words and to try different sounds for the same vowel

Materials

* Word sheet created from template on page 154 for the vowel you are focusing on; see chart on page 140 for suggested words

* Copies of three-column sorting mat on page 156; label columns with the key words that represent the various sounds for that vowel

* Glue and scissors

Sequence

Teach

Begin the lesson like this:

> We are learning to be flexible when we come to a new word. We know that vowels have different sounds and that we need to be ready to try them. Today we are going to focus on the vowel _____ .

The chart on page 140 has words for each vowel for sorting. Over a period of time, do all five lessons, focusing on a different vowel each time. Use the key words that go with each vowel as samples of the sounds each vowel can make in words. Practice saying the key words as a group and emphasize the vowel sound.

Practice

Begin the guided practice like this:

The words in these boxes are mixed up. There are three sounds possible for the vowel __. There may be more sounds for this vowel, but today we will focus on just these three sounds. For each word we will try the three. __, __, and __. If the first sound doesn't make a word, we'll ask, WHAT OTHER SOUND CAN I TRY? and use the next sound or even the third sound if we need to.

Lead the group in a careful reading of the words. When they are ready, have them cut out the words for sorting and glue them down under the key word with the same sound.

Follow Up

Have classroom charts ready, making them up beforehand for each vowel. Put the key words at the top. In reading and writing activities, add more words to each vowel chart under the proper category. Also, have a *No Match* column for the less common sounds of each vowel.

Using What You Know

Prompt for flexibility while reading. If your students try a word, but the wrong vowel sound creates a mismatch, prompt them to ask, WHAT OTHER SOUND CAN I TRY? They should learn to ask themselves this question and refer to the vowel charts you are making as a tool.

Word Categories for Sorting **WHAT OTHER SOUND CAN I TRY?** **SAME VOWEL/DIFFERENT SOUNDS** Use the blank sorting boxes on page 154 to create new word sorts using the same vowel with multiple sounds. Use the key words at the top of each box to represent the various sounds on a blank sorting mat. Stress only the featured vowel and its sounds in each lesson.	**a**			**i**			**u**		
	p<u>a</u>n	**c<u>a</u>ke**	**s<u>a</u>w**	**ch<u>i</u>ck**	**n<u>i</u>ne**	**g<u>i</u>rl**	**b<u>u</u>g**	**c<u>u</u>te**	**p<u>u</u>t**
	black	baby	marker	invent	wide	firm	must	unit	full
	scat	April	father	which	size	thirsty	under	cubic	bush
	strap	taste	star	cinch	fire	birthday	bumps	menu	pull
	splash	stay	stall	little	spider	shirt	trunk	bugle	sugar
	ask	main	squawk	his	lion	first	tubs	human	butcher
	e			**o**					
	sh<u>e</u>ll	**m<u>ea</u>t**	**h<u>e</u>r**	**s<u>o</u>ck**	**sm<u>o</u>ke**	**c<u>o</u>re**			
	elf	zebra	mother	on	open	short			
	them	screech	afternoon	cannot	go	horse			
	spelling	read	winter	cloth	hope	store			
	help	she	camera	box	coat	orbit			
	endless	tree	wonderful	jobs	yellow	fork	Note: Pronunciation of vowel sounds can differ based on regional dialects. Feel free to adapt these lessons.		

Constructing Words From Their Parts

GRADE: 1–2	TIME: 15–20 minutes

FOCUS: To write words from their parts and to bring attention to the embedded letters and vowel chunks

Materials

* Paper
* Pencils
* Chart paper or whiteboard and markers
* Highlighter pens

Sequence

Teach

Begin the lesson like this:

> You are learning to read longer words. One way to read a longer, trickier word is to chunk it. Did you know that each syllable or part in a word has a chunk? Let's try some of your names. Let's clap Jessica's name and see how many parts there are. (Clap <u>Jes-si-ca</u> as you chant it with the students.) Now we should write it and look for three chunks. To be a chunk, it has to have at least one vowel and, usually, other letters.

Write Jes si ca.

> Let's highlight the chunk in each syllable. Remember, in each word or part of a word, the chunk starts with a vowel and goes to the end of the syllable or word.

Lead them in underlining J*es* s*i* c*a*. They will probably be surprised that the chunk can be a single vowel because they are used to working with larger groups of letters.

You already know that every word has to have a vowel. But the truth is, every <u>syllable</u> *in a word has to have a vowel. When we read words, we can look for the vowel chunks, and when we write words, we can build them by syllables with vowel chunks.*

Practice

Begin the guided practice like this:

I will say a word for you to write. But first, we'll clap it to see how many parts to build. Then you'll write the first part, or syllable—and remember, each part must have at least one vowel. Leave a small space after the first syllable; then we'll clap the other parts before writing them.

As you do each word, build it syllable by syllable. When the word is done, model building it on your chart paper. Then model how to highlight the chunk in each syllable—the first vowel in each syllable to the end of the syllable. Use the following words for practice; remember to use each one in a sentence or explain what it means.

re s**ent**   m**on** st**er**   s**ock** et   f**ast** est   h**elp** f**ul**

p**ump** k**in**   s**ub** tr**act**   s**is** t**er**

Follow Up

For another lesson, or as a challenge after the practice, do three-syllable words:

ba nan a   w**on** d**er** f**ul**   el e ph**ant**

f**an** t**as** t**ic**   m**arsh** m**al** l**ow**

Using What You Know

In an independent word center, have students write each other's names by syllable and highlight the vowel pattern or chunk in each syllable. They can copy the spelling of each name then rewrite it and leave spaces to show syllable breaks.

Taking Words Apart in Reading *

GRADE: 1–2   **TIME:** before and during an ongoing reading lesson with each group

FOCUS: To read unknown, often multisyllabic words in stories and to become flexible in taking words apart using known parts

Materials

* Appropriate-level reading materials
* *Nathan & Nicholas Alexander* by Lulu Delacre, Scholastic, 1986 (recommended)
* Chart paper or whiteboard and pens
* Small sticky notes

Sequence

Teach

Begin the lesson like this:

> When we read our story today, we will come to new words that we will need to take apart quickly so that we can keep on reading. We will LOOK INTO THE WORD. We will sometimes ask, WHAT DO I KNOW? and WHAT OTHER SOUND CAN I TRY? All our strategies can help us on tricky words. Here is a word from our story. (<u>Nathan & Nicholas Alexander</u>)

Write *introduce.*

> Everyone should LOOK INTO THE WORD. Ask yourself, WHAT DO I KNOW?

---

* Taking Words Apart in Reading is based on Marie Clay's Taking Words Apart While Reading found in her basic book *Reading Recovery*, 2000.

Lead students through quickly chunking the word. The *duce* may give some students trouble because of the soft sound of c. This is a good opportunity to have them ask, WHAT OTHER SOUND CAN I TRY? They must be flexible with letter combinations, especially vowels.

Good readers take the word apart quickly, make sure the word always makes sense with the story, and go on reading. Here is a huge word from the end of the story. Don't be scared because a word is big; you can take it apart.

Write extraordinary.

> *Are you already LOOKING INTO THE WORD? Who sees something they know? Let's try it!*

Lead the group in blending the word by chunks. If needed, prompt for WHAT OTHER SOUND CAN I TRY?

Practice

Begin the guided practice like this:

> *When you read today, I will be looking and listening for how you TAKE WORDS APART IN READING. I am giving everyone two small sticky notes. Put one by a word you work out, and then keep reading. We will go back when we are done reading, and you can tell us how you took the words apart. The sticky notes will help you find those words fast.*

Follow Up

After all students are done (some may read the book more than once while you listen and coach others), invite them to find their sticky notes and tell how they took the word apart. You can write the word on chart paper or a whiteboard for all to see. Always ask what strategies they used.

Using What You Know

Prompt for these strategies during modeled and guided reading and while listening to individuals read.

Word Sliders With Complex Chunks

GRADE: 1–2 **TIME:** 15–20 minutes to make materials; 10–15 minutes to teach task (this can be a two-day lesson and later be put in an independent work center

FOCUS: To match beginning blends and digraphs (onsets) with more complex vowel chunks (rimes), especially long vowel patterns, and to learn to generate word families and sort out real and made-up words

Materials

* Scissors, tape, a small envelope for each student and staplers
* Consonants blends and digraphs, page 147
* Complex chunk cards, page 110
* Scratch paper or personal Word Books and pencils
* *The Scholastic Rhyming Dictionary* by Sue Young (Scholastic Inc., 1994) (recommended)
* Small sticky notes

Run a copy of the consonants blends and digraphs sheet for each student on card stock. Cut apart the three columns, and tape them into one long vertical strip, making a slider (see page 116 for a description of a vertical slider).

Run a copy of the complex chunk cards for each student on card stock. Have them cut carefully along the lines to make individual cards. Make a pile of chunks with the same vowel at the beginning: *a*, *e*, *i*, and *o*. Continue with a pile for each vowel until you have four piles. (Since there are no common chunks starting with *u*, it is not used in this lesson.)

As students finish, have them read independently while you and trusted helpers staple the chunk cards. Put a staple in the top right corner of each pile so that the chunks can be

folded back to show other patterns for word making. Students can keep their chunk cards in a small envelope with their name on it.

Sequence

Teach

Begin the lesson like this:

> *I want to show you how to use the sliders to make lots of words. I hold the slider with the consonants in my left hand; then I take my chunk cards and turn to the one I want to use. Today I will use <u>ake</u>. I will start at the top of the consonants with the <u>sh</u> and see if that makes a word with <u>ake</u>. /sh/ + /ake/ = /shake/. Now I have to see if /shake/ is a real word. What is <u>shake</u>?*

Discuss multiple meanings. To *shake* hands, *shake* with fear, or as a noun, a *shake* that you drink, like a milkshake. Continue with /thake/, /chake/, /whake/, /blake/, and so forth. Students will need lots of help figuring out the Dr. Seuss words. At first they will think that if they can say it and it rhymes, it must be a word. Question them: "What is a *thake*?" "What is a *chake*?" Tell them that *Blake* is a name.

Practice

Put students in small groups to practice a pattern you give them, such as *eat*. They should slide it down the side of the consonant blends and then discuss if that makes a word. If they agree it is a real word (not a made-up rhyming word), they can record it on their scratch paper or in their word books. Doing this together helps them to sort out real (*flake*) and made-up (*glake*) words. They will get some of these mixed up, but you can circulate among them to help. Even made-up words give them sound-blending practice. You can have groups compare the words they've written down.

Follow Up

Show students how these simple patterns can make larger compound and multi-syllabic words. They can add *ing, er,* and *ed* for example, to many words (*dicing*). Come up with your own examples or look up a pattern in *The Scholastic Rhyming Dictionary*. Do this often so they don't think *ight* is just for *fight*; it can also be found in *frightening*.

Using What You Know

Look for words that come up in guided and shared reading lessons that have these complex chunk patterns. Refer to the chunk cards as another link to these common word families.

sh	fl	st
th	pl	sk
ch	sl	sm
wh	sn	tw
bl	sw	dr
cl	sp	br
gl	sc	cr

ake	ain	ail
eat	ate	ame
ight	ide	ice
ore	oke	ine

Appendix

Mary	had
a	little
lamb.	Its

Word Learning Word Making Word Sorting: 50 Lessons for Success *Scholastic Professional Books*

fleece

was

white

as

snow.

My
Word Book

By _____

Word Learning Word Making Word Sorting: 50 Lessons for Success   Scholastic Professional Books, page 151

Word Solvers Tool Kit:

Super Reader

- Look across the word

- What do I know?

- Chunk the word

- Look into the word

- What other sound can I try?

Word Learning Word Making Word Sorting: 50 Lessons for Success Scholastic Professional Books, page 152

Word Learning Word Making Word Sorting: 50 Lessons for Success   *Scholastic Professional Books*

Sources for Word Work

Pocket Chart Rack for Word Making

You can buy a garment rack on wheels. They are in the ironing board section of stores like Target, Walmart, and K-Mart and are designed for hanging ironing. You can hang a pocket chart on each side with large key rings (one for poetry and one for word making) and move it around your classroom wherever needed.

Highlighter Tape

This tape comes in neon colors that are transparent. Make sure you buy the *reusable* tape so that it comes right up after laying it on a word or word pattern in a book or chart. This can be found at teacher supply stores or from:

Resources for Reading   1-800-ART-READ
Teaching Resource Center 1-800-833-3389

Clear Translucent Counter Chips

These lightly colored transparent plastic chips are about the size of a nickel. They can be used to lay over a word or word part in a book. They "highlight" the part, making it "pop out" and draw student's attention to the exact part of the word you want them to notice. You can also give them to your students and when they stop on an unknown word, prompt "Show me what you know." When students start using the parts they know, they can unlock many more words through analogy. There are enough in a package to share between several teachers.

Resources for Reading   1-800-ART-READ

Wikki Stix

Wikki stix are wax coated yarn that will stick to a book or chart and then peel right off leaving no residue. They are great for framing a word or word chunk for a group to see. Students can be given one during independent center time to be a "word detective"—circle or underline a word and then record it in a personal word book, peel it off and continue searching. These can be found at teacher supply stores or from:

Resources for Reading   1-800-ART-READ
Teaching Resource Center 1-800-833-3389

Individual Magnetic Boards

Look in the housewares department of stores like Target, Walmart, and K-Mart. Burner covers are sold to keep grease off your stove's burners, but they make great individual magnetic boards for word making with magnetic letters. Small cookie sheets serve the same purpose but may be more expensive.

Pocket Chart Highlighters

This is bright, translucent, thick material that is perfect for highlighting words or word parts in a pocket chart or big book. You can use is to make translucent letter and word frames (see template on page 54) for highlighting a word or word chunk in a lesson. Because it is transparent, students can see the rest of the word you are highlighting but focus through the cut out window on the key part you want to emphasize.

Teaching Resource Center 1-800-833-3389

References

Allington, Richard, & Cunningham, Patricia, *Schools That Work: Where All Children Learn to Read and Write*, New York: Harper Collins, 1997.

Bear, Donald, Invernizzi, Marcia, Johnston, Francine, & Templeton, Shane, *Words Their Way: Word Study for Phonics, Vocabulary, and Spelling Instruction*, Upper Saddle River, N.J.: Merrill/Prentice-Hall, 1996.

Bureau of Education and Research provides professional videos of Judy Lynch modeling these and other word strategies. Contact them at 1-800-736-2136 for a brochure.

Clay, Marie, *An Observation Survey of Early Literacy Achievement*. Portsmouth, NH: Heinemann Educational Books, 1993.

Clay, Marie, *Becoming Literate: The Construction of Inner Control*. Portsmouth, NH: Heinemann Educational Books, 1991.

Clay, Marie, *Reading Recovery: A Guidebook for Teachers in Training*, Portsmouth: Heinemann, 1993.

Cunningham, Patricia, *California Reader*, Vol 34 No 1, p.30, California Reading Association publication.

Cunningham, Patricia, *Phonics They Use*, New York, N.Y.: Harper Collins, 1995.

Eeds, M. "Bookwords: Using a Beginning Word List of High Frequency Words From Children's Literature K–3," *The Reading Teacher*, January 1985.

Ehri, L.C., "Development of the Ability to Read Words" in Barr, R., Kamil, M.R., Mosenthal,P., & Pearson, P.D. (Eds.) *Handbook of Reading Research*, Vol. II. New York: Longman, 1996.

Ehri, L.C., "Phases of Word Learning: Implications for Instruction with Delayed and Disabled Readers," *Reading Research Quarterly*, April-June 1998.

Ehri, L.C., & Wilce, L.S. "Does Learning to Spell Help Beginners Learn to Read Words?" *Reading Research Quarterly*, 22, 1985, 47-65.

Fountas, Irene, & Pinnell, Gay Su, "How and Why Children Learn about Sounds, Letters, and Words in Reading Recovery Lessons," *The Running Record*, Fall 1999, vol 12, no 1.

Fry, E., Kress, J., and Fountoukidis, D., (1993) *The Reading Teacher's Book of Lists*, 3rd Ed., West Nyack, New York, The Center for Applied Research in Education.

Gaskins, I., and Ehri, L., "Procedures for Word Learning: Making Discoveries About Words," *The Reading Teacher*, Dec 96–Jan 97, Vol 50, No 4, pp. 312-326.

Goswami, U., & Bryant, P., *Phonological Skills and Learning to Read*, Hillsdale: Lawrence Erlbaum, 1990.

Lynch, Judy, *Easy Lessons for Teaching Word Families*, New York: Scholastic, 1998.

Michel, P. *The Child's View of Reading: Understandings for Teachers and Parents*, Boston: Allyn & Bacon, 1994.

Neal, Judith, "Teaching for Visual/Word Analysis," West Coast Conference of Reading Recovery, March 6, 1999.

Pinnell, GaySu, & Fountas, Irene, *Word Matters, Teaching Phonics and Spelling in the Reading/Writing Classroom*, Portsmouth, N.H.: Heinemann, 1998.

Rayner,K., & Pollatsek, A., *The Psychology of Reading*, Engelwood Cliffs, N.J.: Prentice Hall, 1989.

Sitton, Rebecca, Spelling Sourcebook I, Northwest Textbook Depository, 1-800-676-6630 (This sourcebook provides the whole program which uses the high frequency word lists as a starting place for direct instruction in all the basic spelling skills and the introduction to many other words needed for spelling).

Wagstaff, Janiel, *Teaching Reading and Writing With Word Walls*, New York: Scholastic, 1999.

Young, Sue, *The Scholastic Rhyming Dictionary*, New York: Scholastic, 1994.